The Management Training Tool Kit

35 Exercises to Prepare Managers for th Challenges They Face Every Day

The Management Training Tool Kit

35 Exercises to Prepare Managers for the Challenges They Face Every Day

Alan Clardy, Ph.D.

AMACOM

New York • Atlanta • Brussels • Chicago • Mexico City • San Francisco
Shanghai • Tokyo • Toronto • Washington, D.C.

This publication is designed to provide accurate and authoritative information in regard to the subject matter covered. It is sold with the understanding that the publisher is not engaged in rendering legal, accounting, or other professional service. If legal advice or other expert assistance is required, the services of a competent professional person should be sought.

Library of Congress Cataloging-in-Publication Data

Clardy, Alan B.
    The management training tool kit : 35 exercises to prepare managers for the challenges they face every day / Alan Clardy.
       p. cm.
    Includes index.
    ISBN 978-0-8144-3114-6
    1. Executives—Training of—Case studies. 2. Management—Study and teaching—Case studies. 3. Management—Case studies. 4. Supervision of employees—Study and teaching—Psychological aspects. I. Title.
    HD30.4.C567 2012
    658.4'07124—dc23
                                      2011047827

About AMA

American Management Association (www.amanet.org) is a world leader in talent development, advancing the skills of individuals to drive business success. Our mission is to support the goals of individuals and organizations through a complete range of products and services, including classroom and virtual seminars, webcasts, webinars, podcasts, conferences, corporate and government solutions, business books and research. AMA's approach to improving performance combines experiential learning—learning through doing—with opportunities for ongoing professional growth at every step of one's career journey.

Printing number
10 9 8 7 6 5 4 3 2 1

Contents

Contents

PDF files for the handouts for Case Study descriptions as well as other files
are available to purchasers of this book at:
www.amacombooks.org/go/ManagementTraining

Handouts

www.amacombooks.org/go/ManagementTraining

Handouts

Appendixes

ACKNOWLEDGMENTS

The following individuals deserve recognition for their contributions to this book.

First, I would like to extend my gratitude to Robert W. Carkhuff, the original publisher of this book. Bob was visionary enough to see the potential for these cases, willing enough to risk trying out an untried author, and patient enough to give him some extra time to finish the project. I want to thank Bob for his help in making this volume possible.

Second, I am indebted to the numerous managers and supervisors who were willing to share their stories with me, to let me listen to the troubles, frustrations, and, yes, the mistakes they inherited from their predecessors. In these moments, it was happily unclear who was the trainer and who was the student. Their experiences have given all of us an opportunity to learn, and on our behalf, I wish to thank them.

Using the Cases in This Book

The cases reported in this book are, with few exceptions, based on true stories that I have gathered from a broad spectrum of supervisors and managers. While the essential features of each story have been retained, the names of the people and organizations have been changed to protect their identities, as well as to make the cases more flexible for training purposes.

I have used these cases successfully in various management and supervisory training programs over the years. From my experience, I have found that they produce recognition, discussion, and even debate. Invariably, they challenge trainees and encourage them to rethink and reexamine the fundamentals of being an effective leader. Together, as presented in this manual, they cover a full range of management and supervisory issues and concerns.

Although the cases are written primarily in the context of service industries, with a few cases set in the manufacturing industries, they go straight to the heart of universal leadership challenges, and their application extends into virtually any organizational area. They include such issues as dealing with a difficult employee, improving performance, training and coaching, selecting the right person for the job, and managing fairly and effectively. These challenges are likely to confront any manager or supervisor in any kind of organization, and developing the ability to respond to them productively and to learn from them is what this book is all about.

The Case Studies in This Book

The Cases

Many of the cases are presented in one complete story; others are subdivided into sections that highlight major decision points in the development of the story. Suggested questions for discussion or assignment follow each section or are at the end of the case.

Case Discussion

Accompanying each case is the Case Discussion. This helpful guide contains a summary of the case, along with answers to the suggested questions presented in the body of the case. The Case Discussion attachment is intended for use by the trainer or discussion facilitator.

Case Issues Index

The Case Issues Index lists the cases and the major management and supervisory issues addressed in each (see page xxi). Use the index to locate the issue you want to cover; then read the case summary in the Case Discussion to learn the specifics.

Using Case Studies in Training Programs

There are several ways by which you can profitably include case studies as part of your training programs. These options are reviewed below.

Preparing for the Training Program

Putting sufficient effort into the preclass preparation process can make the difference between a focused, effective training session and a fragmentary, inconsequential one. As a regular practice, I require managers and supervisors who will be participating in my training programs to submit a case report drawn from their personal experience as part of this preparation process. There are several reasons for doing so:

1. Case write-ups serve as a needs assessment, revealing the issues and concerns of the people who are coming into the program.

2. Case preparation begins the process of orienting the participants to the training.

3. For the cases selected, learning materials specific to the client organization and its unique management needs can be prepared and used in the training.

A Case Report Worksheet designed for the preclass case assignment is provided for your use at the conclusion of this introductory section (see page xv). You can distribute this worksheet to participants some time before the scheduled start date. Participants return their completed forms to you. You look for cases that seem representative and important, and then write a case based on that information for use in the training.

The Training Session

To use either the cases provided here or ones that you develop as part of the training, select a case(s) that fits the topic under study.

In the training session, the participants are organized into leaderless groups, and the cases are distributed. The groups are given anywhere from 10 to 30 minutes to read and discuss the case. When the participants are ready, debriefing is conducted, beginning with a prompt recitation of the story's main facts. This review leads directly into the questions supplied at the end of the case.

Case discussions are important features of the training and serve two functions: First, they promote participant involvement, encouraging participants to talk and interact with one another; second, they offer marvelous opportunities for participants to apply and extend what they have learned to specific problems. The productivity of these case discussions can be increased by reviewing the steps in Analyzing a Case, page xvii, or by providing each participant with a Case Analysis Guidelines Worksheet (see page xix). These worksheets help participants evaluate the cases and apply their problem-solving skills to each group consensus on case solutions.

Cases and Role Playing

In many of the cases, a meeting between the manager/supervisor and the employee(s) is needed. Several different kinds of goals are possible for such a meeting: to communicate decisions, to listen for information, to negotiate a solution, to chastise, or to recognize good work. In this context, these cases present natural gateways for role-playing practice exercises.

To use these exercises as a lead in to role-playing, the trainer assigns to participants the various roles of supervisor, employee, or anyone else integral to the case. Then, the participants are given the task of conducting the meeting already discussed by the group. The case establishes the situation, but how the role players, especially those in supervisory roles, deal with the situation is up to them.

The participant who plays the role of the supervisor usually has the most control over how the situation develops—and the most decisions to make. For example, if the scenario is a disciplinary meeting, what should the supervisor say? And, how should he or she act? While there might be common-sense rules about proper action, the use of more specific behavioral guidelines is often desirable.

There are numerous sources of behavioral guidelines that are appropriate for use in case scenario role plays. Some behavior-modeling training programs provide a list of steps a manager should take in any given situation; thus, a set of behavior principles for coaching can be applied in these situations. Guidelines may also be drawn from the general literature. The behaviors associated with assertive communication, for example, are rather widely known and can be used as the basis for training and role-playing activities. Finally, keep in mind that the organization that employs the participants may itself be an invaluable source of guidance. The organization's policies and procedures in disciplinary matters, for instance, may clearly indicate what a supervisor should do and say, thereby providing the role player with an established model of conduct for dealing with disciplinary problems.

The cases, which create the context for action and the role-playing exercises, bring participants into the sphere of action and help them further develop problem-solving and decision-making skills. Using these cases in conjunction with role-playing exercises and the appropriate guidelines can thus result in a highly effective training method.

Questions and Answers About the Cases

How Were These Cases Developed?

These cases, collected over the past 10 years, are based on the experiences of managers and supervisors in a variety of professions. The occupational environments represented here include financial, health-care, educational, governmental, retail, and manufacturing settings.

Each case tells the story of a particularly compelling or challenging management and supervisory situation. Representing the "critical incidents" in the lives of managers and supervisors, these stories have been generated by the kind of circumstances that, whether simply unusual or quite extraordinary, can have profound effects on individuals and organizations. They are also circumstances for which clear-cut rules and routine procedures do not always apply.

Because the cases were developed according to the accounts of real-life circumstances, there often is neither one absolutely correct answer nor a single correct course of action to follow that will neatly solve the problems they pose. Such realistic difficulties only increase the power of these cases as learning tools. When a case situation can support several different possible responses, it promotes discussion and stimulates competing opinions and alternative points of view. Case discussions, in turn, promote the evaluations of options and help build judgment in considering how to handle difficult leadership situations.

A Note on Leadership Orientation

Several of these cases were developed for use with training in situation leadership methods. *Situational leadership* is an approach to directing employees in which the type of appropriate leadership style depends in large part on the maturity level of the employees. For instance, according to this method, a highly competent employee should not be managed in the same way that an untrained, poorly motivated new employee is managed: a supervisor or manager should use a more individualized style of leadership.

xiii

The classic statement of this approach is given by Paul Hershey and Kenneth Blanchard in *Management of Organizational Behavior: Utilizing Human Resources.*

Where Did the Answers to the Case Studies Come From?

The answers provided in the supplementary Case Discussion sections are based on my experience in managing employees, in training managers and supervisors, and in administering human resource management systems. Others may see the cases in different ways and recommend courses of action that vary from those that I have recommended. Case discussion will often yield a wealth of opinions that, through case analysis, can be developed into several options for resolving the case; then, the "best" alternative from among those options can be chosen (see page xvii, Analyzing a Case: A General Strategy). Again, equally competent managers and supervisors may arrive at different—yet equally plausible—solutions.

Can the Cases Be Adapted to My Organization?

If necessary, you can adapt and customize these cases by changing the identity of the firm and/or industry while retaining the essential features of the story. For example, with very little effort, you can shift the setting of a case from healthcare to finance by just changing names and some slight details. "Data processing" in a hospital could be translated into "information systems" in a bank, for instance, in order to fine-tune the case to your specific situation.

I do *not* recommend, though, using the name of your organization in the case. By using your firm's name, you invite participants to make analogies and speculate on whom this case is really about, and it would not be unusual for rumors to start. Moreover, the important issues of the case can become secondary to these distractions.

For similar reasons, I also do not recommend using the names of public figures, whether real or fictional, for case characters. If a boss is named Michael Scott (in *The Office*) or an employee Sue Sylvester (in *Glee*), participants will immediately apply the character traits of those fictional personalities to the individuals in the case, which, again, distracts participants from a full consideration of the case issues.

Case Report Worksheet ✍

Please answer each of the items on the form below. Certain cases will be adapted for use in training. If your case is selected for use, you will be contacted for your permission to use it and, if permission is given, for more details. The case prepared for final use will be written so that all people involved, including yourself, will be anonymous.

Name: _____   Work phone: _____

Describe a challenging situation you have faced or are currently facing as a supervisor. There are several reasons why the situation may be challenging:

- It was unusual.
- Even though it was unusual, you were not sure what to do about it.
- The demands or conditions were complicated.

There could be other reasons. The situation could be a problem or an opportunity. It might involve an individual or a group you manage directly, or someone you do not manage at all. Use the reverse of this page or attach additional paper if you need more writing space.

1. Identify the people who were involved: use job titles (no names) and describe each person's age, gender, years in current position, and/or any other relevant characteristics.

   _____

   _____

   _____

   _____

   _____

2. Describe the nature of the situation. What is going on? What is happening? What is the performance issue?

   _____

   _____

   _____

   _____

   _____

The Management Training Tool Kit: 35 Exercises to Prepare Managers for the Challenges They Face Every Day, ©2012 HRD Press.
Published by AMACOM Books, American Management Association, www.amanet.org.

3. What was your role? What did you do? What happened?

_____

_____

_____

_____

_____

4. What was the conclusion, or what is the current status?

_____

_____

_____

_____

_____

Return to: _____   By: _____

The Management Training Tool Kit: 35 Exercises to Prepare Managers for the Challenges They Face Every Day, ©2012 HRD Press.
Published by AMACOM Books, American Management Association, www.amanet.org.

Analyzing a Case: A General Strategy

A case is a story that describes a problematic incident, event, or situation. It typically reports in-depth information about certain aspects of the situation while underreporting others, and its conclusion is commonly left open-ended. The mission of the case analysis is to make sense of the given material and to identify appropriate actions for handling the situation.

Successful case discussions begin with an analysis of the key issues in the case. This analysis then serves as the basis for defining the most desirable outcomes and considering what options are available. This process usually results in a diversity of opinions, as participants view the case situation from their individual perspectives, stressing different values and promoting different outcomes. Such diversity of opinion is the strength of the group case exercise. Participants should value these differences, recognizing them as essential to learning, and make a special effort to encourage new opinions about the case. As a result, the case exercise will become an even more profitable learning experience.

In case analysis, participants also evaluate the different opinions about the case and use their evaluations as the basis for forming a common opinion. By working together in this way to build group consensus on case solutions, participants gain a deeper understanding of how they can constructively deal with real-life leadership issues. Included below are case analysis guidelines that constitute a seven-step method for reaching group consensus. These steps provide participants with a common source of direction for addressing case issues and also appear in the form of a handy Case Analysis Guidelines Worksheet at the conclusion of this section (see page xix).

Case Analysis Guidelines

Step 1. *What are the key issues or problems of the case?*

Any case may suggest several interpretations of what the focal concerns are. It is helpful to begin by identifying as many different interpretations as possible. Have each participant state why he or she identified the issues or problems as key.

Step 2. *Prioritize the problems.*

Participants should focus on the key issues of the case. This may involve selecting one of the issues already raised or creating a new statement that identifies the problem. In some cases, there may be several problems at work, in which case participants may wish to simply rank the problems in terms of either potential importance or timing of impact.

Step 3. *Consider whether it is necessary to determine the "cause" of the problem.*

In some cases, it is important to determine what caused the problem in order to identify the appropriate solution(s). In other cases, the cause of the problem is not as important as what to do about it. Therefore, when working on a case, always ask whether it is necessary to decide what the cause is.

It should be noted that speculating on the motivations of the individuals in a case seldom does more than sidetrack a case study. By training to determine why a person acted in a certain way, participants can easily fall into unproductive discussions that revolve around guesswork instead of focusing on the situation at hand. Managers and supervisors often must respond to actions (or lack of actions) made by the people with whom they work, and reflecting on the motivations of others is, in this regard, only a diversion.

Step 4. *Brainstorm the options available to the leader.*

There is always one option: Do nothing. However, there are usually several ways to respond to a problem, and helping participants identify those options is an important part of case discussions. Participants should be encouraged to use their best brainstorming skills to determine what the options are.

Step 5. *Evaluate the options.*

Each option will have advantages and disadvantages. In management and human resource issues, there are several criteria that may be useful for evaluating different options, including:

- The power of the option to solve the problem
- The impact of the option on organizational performance and/or morale
- Legal or regulatory liabilities and requirements
- Cost of the option
- The ability of the person(s) involved to carry out the option (in terms of skill, authority, or basic motivation)

Step 6. *Select the optimum solution.*

The ideal solution will produce the best outcome at the least cost. In management situations, this may not be possible. Therefore, selecting the best solution may involve balancing competing opportunities and constraints with an optimum solution that produces satisfactory outcomes on as many criteria as possible.

Step 7. *Describe how the solution should be implemented.*

Create a plan or "script" of what the manager or supervisor should do to implement the solution.

Case Analysis Guidelines Worksheet ✍

1. What are the key issues or problems of the case?

   _____

   _____

   _____

2. Prioritize the issues or problems.

   1) _____

   2) _____

   3) _____

3. Is it necessary to identify the cause of the problem?

   _____

   _____

   _____

4. Brainstorm the options available.

   _____

   _____

   _____

5. Evaluate the options: Advantages: Disadvantages:

   • _____   _____   _____

   • _____   _____   _____

   • _____   _____   _____

6. Select the optimum solution.

   _____

   _____

7. Describe how the solution should be implemented.

   _____

   _____

   _____

The Management Training Tool Kit: 35 Exercises to Prepare Managers for the Challenges They Face Every Day, ©2012 HRD Press.
Published by AMACOM Books, American Management Association, www.amanet.org.

Case Issues Index

xxi

The Management Training Tool Kit

35 Exercises to Prepare Managers for the Challenges They Face Every Day

The 35 Case Studies

Case 1 ✍

How Come They Make More Than I Do?

Background Information

Fran Jefferson began her job as the supervisor of the Training Department of Metro Bank and Trust Company almost four years ago. She was generally pleased with the four trainers and one secretary in her unit. Indeed, Fran took pride in her ability to create a high-morale and high-performance unit. This was particularly pleasing to Fran because they were constantly busy and barely able to keep up with the volume of training expected from them.

Then, early on Wednesday morning, Fran's secretary, Judy Martin, knocked on Fran's door and asked to see her. Fran liked Judy and considered the secretary to be one of her "stars." Indeed, in an effort to develop Judy's talents and abilities, Fran had gone out of her way to give Judy special assignments, including her in all the major planning activities of the department and entrusting her with the administration of certain departmental programs, such as tuition assistance and evaluation follow-through. By now, Judy functioned more as an administrative aide than as a secretary.

It was clear that Judy was upset about something as she seated herself in the chair next to Fran's desk. Slowly, Judy placed a job-posting application form in front of Fran. She would not look her supervisor in the eyes.

Fran was surprised, to say the least. As far as Fran knew, Judy liked both her job and working in the Training Department. In turn, everyone else in the department liked and respected Judy.

Fran looked over the form and said casually, "So you want to post for the executive secretary job in the Branch Management Division." She paused. "Could I ask you for some additional information, Judy? I'm kind of surprised."

Judy looked at her clasped hands, thinking. Fran waited.

Finally, Judy looked up and said: "I noticed in last week's job posting that the executive secretary position is graded as a 14. Now that's two grades higher than my job!"

She caught her breath. "You know my friend Mary Johnson works over there. She told me that half the time the secretary sits around doing nothing."

Judy continued, gathering some anger in her look and resentment in her voice. "Look, Fran, you know how hard I work, how hard we all work, around here. I mean, I'm always busy. I don't see why I should work in a job graded at a 12 and work twice as hard and yet not be paid the same as that secretary. The requirements for the job are just a little higher than mine, and the merit raise you gave me last month hardly helped at all."

Fran listened, then she replied: "It sounds to me, Judy, that you're feeling angry because you think you should be paid more for the work you do and that you want to switch jobs rather than put up with things as they are. Am I right?"

Judy nodded her head in agreement.

1

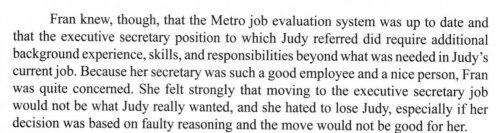

Fran knew, though, that the Metro job evaluation system was up to date and that the executive secretary position to which Judy referred did require additional background experience, skills, and responsibilities beyond what was needed in Judy's current job. Because her secretary was such a good employee and a nice person, Fran was quite concerned. She felt strongly that moving to the executive secretary job would not be what Judy really wanted, and she hated to lose Judy, especially if her decision was based on faulty reasoning and the move would not be good for her.

Fran tried to figure out what to do.

CASE QUESTIONS

1. What are the reasons given by Judy Martin for wanting to post for a position in another department? Which points are accurate and which are debatable?

2. How should Fran respond to Judy's request to transfer?

3. How should Fran respond to Judy's salary complaints?

The Management Training Tool Kit: 35 Exercises to Prepare Managers for the Challenges They Face Every Day, ©2012 HRD Press.
Published by AMACOM Books, American Management Association, www.amanet.org.

Case Discussion:
How Come They Make More Than I Do?

Summary

Fran Jefferson supervised the Training Department of Metro Bank. One of her star employees, Judy Martin, surprised Fran one day with a job-posting application. Judy wanted to transfer to another department where the employees made more money (in higher evaluated jobs) and supposedly did less work. In the ensuing discussion, Fran learned that Judy was very unhappy with the merit increase she had recently received. Judy believed she could earn more money in the open position, which was three grades higher than the position she currently occupied.

Judy now functioned more as an administrative assistant than as the departmental secretary (the position for which she had been hired). Fran knew that the job evaluation system in use was valid and up-to-date, and that grade differences between Judy's job and the open position meant real differences in responsibility, skill, and accountability.

Fran did not want to lose Judy.

Answers to Case Questions

1. **What are the reasons given by Judy Martin for wanting to post for a position in another department? Which points are accurate and which are debatable?**

Judy's line of reasoning is as follows:

(a) Her recent merit increase was not adequate enough reward for her hard work.
   This is Judy's opinion, and for her, it is true.

(b) There is an open position that would pay much more than what she is making now.
   It is true that this open position would pay her more than she is making now.

(c) She has heard that the job in question is easier to do than the one she has now.
   Unfortunately, this point is misleading and probably wrong. Her information is based on hearsay. In fact, grade differences of three levels mean these jobs require higher levels of talent, initiative, and responsibility. Judy has confused being busy with working at a higher level of difficulty.

(d) Therefore, she wants to get an easier, higher paying job by moving to that new position.
   She might get a higher paying job, but it would not likely be an easier job.

2. **How should Fran respond to Judy's request to transfer?**

In many job-posting systems, the posting employee is required to notify his or her supervisor of the intention to post for a position. However, the employee is not required to obtain the supervisor's permission. To the extent that this rule applies here, Fran cannot do anything but pass along the posting application.

3

However, it would be prudent of Fran to help Judy make the best career decision in this manner. While agreeing to move the job-posting application along, Fran should also counsel Judy. First, she should encourage Judy to do some career and job informational interviewing. For example, Judy should be encouraged to meet with people in the other department to learn what they really do. Second, she needs to think about what she wants in a job. Finally, Fran should explain to Judy that the jobs are graded differently because there are real and significant differences in the jobs. She should caution Judy that hearsay can be misleading and that she should look at the executive secretary position in terms of levels of skills and accountability, not just in terms of dollar differences.

3. How should Fran respond to Judy's salary complaints?

It is likely that Judy is motivated in part by her anger and resentment over what she sees as an inadequate recognition of her hard work. Fran should work to communicate her appreciation for Judy's contributions. In addition, Fran needs to note that Judy is performing a job that is higher than the job for which she was hired. Judy should institute a job re-evaluation request.

Case 2 ✍

"She's a Smart Enough Broad"

Background Information

The young man glanced at the nameplate on his desk after closing the file cabinet drawer: *James Washington, Center Manager.* He leaned against the cabinet for a moment, smiling and thinking.

James really liked the way that title sounded. And why not? He was only 24 years old, had just completed the company's Management Associate Trainee Program, and had just assumed the manager's job at the Northview Servicing Center. He was eager to do a good job in this first assignment, and there was a lot about the job that he liked. However, there was one thing he didn't like, and he could see her through the glass partition of his office out on the service center's main floor.

His problem was Dorothy Rogers or, more exactly, the way he felt about her. In his opinion, she was both pushing and resisting him.

Dorothy was something of an established figure at Northview, having worked there for over 12 years as an assistant manager. She was now 59 years old and had dropped hints occasionally about retiring. "If only…," James thought to himself.

He remembered the first time he met Dorothy about six weeks ago. James had just learned he was being promoted into the Northview manager's job. He went to visit the service center to meet the personnel and begin the transition process with Hank Waters. Hank was the current manager and was being moved to manage a larger branch of the company closer to his home. He had been at Northview almost two years.

After showing James the facility and introducing some of the sales and service representatives, Hank had walked James to Dorothy's desk and introduced them. Although she was very pleasant and nice, James watched rather uncomfortably as Hank tried to pass along an assignment to her regarding a customer account investigation. Six weeks later, their exchange, which follows, remained clear in James's memory.

Hank: By the way, Dorothy, can you follow up on the Williams's account problem we talked about earlier today? I just got word from downtown that…

Dorothy: (*interrupting in a soft yet determined voice*) Now Hank, you know that if I do that for you, I won't be able to take care of the budget reconcilement report you have me do each week. Don't you think you can take care of it yourself?

Hank: (*pausing a moment, obviously thinking*) Well, yes, I know you're busy. I was just hoping that you could…

5

Dorothy: (*jumping back in, this time with a certain accusatory tone in her voice*) Look, Hank, what do you want me to do? I can't do both. You know I'm busy. (*She stares expectantly at Hank; James looks at her desk, which is neat and clean.*)

Hank: Well, you know… okay, you may be right. Let me go ahead and do it.

Dorothy: (*nodding in agreement*) That's better, I think. Don't you?

Hank had seemed relieved to end the conversation. He walked with James back into his office. Dorothy went to get some coffee.

"She really runs this place," Hank told James. "I hate to impose. She knows so much about all the operational and service matters of this center."

James nodded his head. "I guess she must be pretty important."

Hank hadn't reacted as he sat behind his desk.

James moved back to the chair behind his desk. He continued to look at Dorothy as she finished working with her customer. He thought back to his first few weeks on the job. At first, Dorothy had been fine and, in fact, very helpful. This was perfect because not only did James still have a great deal to learn about Northview's operations, he also had a lot of work to do elsewhere. For example, much of his time was spent outside the service center, meeting existing customers, doing sales calls, attending training, and fulfilling similar obligations. In the month that he had been at Northview, he had spent probably no more than a total of five hours with her.

Unfortunately, most of that time with Dorothy had spent sorting out and listening to a problem between her and senior service associate, Bonnie Johnson. Bonnie was Dorothy's age, but that was about all the two women seemed to have in common, for Bonnie was rather quiet and reserved. James had expressed his interest in Bonnie taking a more active role in working with the other service associates, but Dorothy had not liked that idea, thinking that James was trying to take away some of her job duties. Consequently, she started fighting with Bonnie over any little detail.

James learned about this bickering from comments and meetings with both Dorothy and Bonnie, as well as from some of the center's other service associates. Last Monday, after what seemed like a week of nonstop arguing, he called them both into his office.

"Look, you two," he told them, "I'm really getting tired of all this squabbling. I expect both of you to cooperate and function as a team. I'm the one running the show here. If this fighting doesn't stop, I'll have to put you on probation. And if it doesn't stop after that, I may just fire you."

Shocked and silent, both had left his office without barely a glance in his direction.

After that meeting, Dorothy became quiet, but seemed unmotivated. She appeared to have settled into a low-energy and low-output mode. She would do what she was supposed to do, but nothing more than that. And James had overheard her complaining to other employees, both at Northview and elsewhere, about a number of things, including the company, the service center, and James. He had thought to himself,

The Management Training Tool Kit: 35 Exercises to Prepare Managers for the Challenges They Face Every Day, ©2012 HRD Press.
Published by AMACOM Books, American Management Association, www.amanet.org.

"She's just a negative person. Sure, she's a smart enough broad. She knows how far she can go. But don't expect her to be of any real help."

Upon remembering those thoughts, James leaned back in his chair, rubbing his eyes. He could not argue with that estimation of Dorothy, only confirm it. His mind turned to what had happened at closing yesterday. The memory was so vivid it was as if the events were taking place at that very moment.

The last customer had just left and the doors are locked. Everyone is busy closing their stations when suddenly Dorothy brings out a small portable television, makes herself comfortable at her desk, and turns the television on, clearly intending to watch it.

James, seeing her do this, is dumbfounded. He thinks to himself, "What in the heck is she doing? If my boss comes here, I'm in big trouble." He remembers the recent memo from headquarters, demanding more productivity and application to getting the work done.

He walks over to her desk. She smiles as he approaches and says, "Oh, it's okay, James. We do this every so often. Hank said I could watch it when I had to stay and finish up routine work, as long as I wouldn't let it interfere with the work."

James feels pushed to the limit. He decides not to say anything to her and leaves, certain that at this point she's testing him, trying to find out how far she can go. She is challenging his authority again, he feels, and this time he must do something dramatic.

James was still trying to decide what to do as he watched Dorothy finish with the customer and return to her seat.

CASE QUESTIONS

1. Is there a problem(s) here?

2. What is (are) the problem(s)?

3. What should be done?

The Management Training Tool Kit: 35 Exercises to Prepare Managers for the Challenges They Face Every Day, ©2012 HRD Press.
Published by AMACOM Books, American Management Association, www.amanet.org.

Case Discussion:
"She's a Smart Enough Broad"

Summary

James Washington was a young graduate of the organization's Management Associate Trainee Program. He recently assumed the manager's job at one of the organization's service centers, Northview Servicing. Dorothy Rogers had been an assistant manager at Northview for over 12 years and was more than twice James's age. After a series of encounters with her, James began to feel that Dorothy was resisting his taking over leadership of the service center and was working behind his back to undermine his authority. James threatened to fire her at one point. Subsequently, she became passive and withdrawn. To James's astonishment, one day after the store had closed, she brought out a portable television and placed it on her desk, intending to watch it. This act was in direct violation of company directives. James wondered what to do about the situation.

Answers to Case Questions

1. Is there a problem(s) here?

Yes, there are several problems here.

2. What is (are) the problems?

First, there is the immediate problem of Dorothy violating company rules by bringing out the television.

Second, there is the more deep-seated problem of James need to establish a working relationship with someone with whom he has had difficulty. To complicate matters even more, James is dependent upon Dorothy for help with managing the center because of her expertise and background. Unfortunately, James indicates that he has an attitude and set of assumptions about her that can hamper the establishment of a good working relationship (for example, his derogatory and backhanded compliment that she was a "smart enough broad"). James's limited experience managing others will be a drawback in this respect.

Third, there is the more profound problem of establishing effective control and leadership over the service center.

3. What should be done?

First, it is not too late for James to hold a "transition meeting" with the staff. In this meeting, there is a mutual communication about expectations, styles, and needs. Such a meeting would allow him to detail his performance expectations and management practices, as well as learn more about what employees want and need. Thereafter, he can hold follow-up meetings with each employee individually.

Second, he should ask to talk with Dorothy privately. As part of that session, he should indicate matter-of-factly but firmly that television watching is not acceptable; he should explain why and ask for Dorothy's help. During this meeting, he should also raise the problem of how he has been feeling—that she is pushing and resisting him. In this way, they can establish a more effective working relationship.

James should raise these issues assertively. That is, he should preface his remarks by noting that he is still new to managing and that he will likely make some mistakes. For example, it would be appropriate to apologize for the firing threat made earlier. He should explain his frustrations in trying to find a good working relationship and ask if she has any similar feelings. This approach could be a nonconfrontational way to open up for discussion on how they will work together.

It appears that Dorothy is technically a very competent employee, although her motivation level is average. A participative style of managing is suggested. Thus, a general strategy would be to recognize and capitalize on her technical abilities while trying to improve her motivation. Clearly defined authorities and a regular reporting relationship can help achieve the former, while including her in center planning and decision making can hopefully improve the latter.

James's efforts to redirect the quality of their relationship does not mean, though, that he abdicates center leadership duties. He should spend more time working with both Dorothy and Bonnie Johnson to define and implement any changes in their respective duties. For example, in a discussion with Dorothy, James should state his plan and his rationale as well as ask for her help and suggestions. James should also be attentive to indications that he is failing to establish a workable relation with Dorothy. If there is an inadequate response on her part, he may need to begin either to transfer her, to discipline her, or to terminate her.

Case 3 ✍️

Improving Performance in Business Services

Background Information

Two years ago, the State Department of Economic Development created the Business Services Group to provide special services to out-of-state businesses that were considering relocating in the state. Another key task of the group was to help those businesses that had recently relocated get settled and operating as quickly as possible. In that two-year period, the Business Services Group put together a good record of helping more than 35 businesses move into the state efficiently.

The Business Services Group was staffed with a complement of a department manager and five business development specialists, along with some secretarial and clerical support. The job of the business development specialists consisted principally of contacting and working with appropriate personnel in each business to identify the kinds of information or help they needed, and then making sure that the correct assistance arrived. The specialists also served as "troubleshooters" for the business whenever there were problems with the "bureaucracy." Specialists were responsible for keeping these businesses happy and efficient. As such, the specialists needed to be imaginative, persistent, and self-driven. Each specialist had a quota of contacts and services to make each month.

Charles Thompson was initially made acting supervisor of the Business Services Group after the hasty departure of the previous department manager. After three weeks of keeping things running, he was promoted to manager. Charles originally was hired as a specialist. Six months ago, he was transferred to another related department to serve as assistant manager.

When Charles learned that he was moving back to the Business Services Group, he was very happy because he would be reunited with the people with whom he used to work. In fact, Charles had worked with all five of them to some degree, while he was in Business Services.

John Willis, now the senior specialist, joined the Business Services Group the same day Charles did. In fact, they had come from the same department to join Business Services. Suzy Harris and Barbara Garrett became specialists shortly thereafter. For most of the time that Charles was in the group, these four worked together easily and effectively. As the Business Services Group expanded, Tom Rollins was added. Finally, before Charles transferred, he had a chance to orient and train Melanie Bronson, who had been hired as his replacement.

As a group, these individuals represented a fairly high level of experience in the business services function. Moreover, based on their record sand reputations, they also performed very well. Charles reviewed the batch of complimentary letters sent to the Business Services Group, some of which had been signed by the governor. They worked effectively and creatively on their own with few personnel problems.

11

Case 3: Improving Performance in Business Services

In spite of this consistent record, though, Audrey Downs (Charles's new boss, the head of Economic Development) felt there was still room for improvement. She explained her thinking to Charles in a luncheon meeting one day, not long after Charles had been promoted to manager. By that time, Charles had seen enough of the Business Service Group's operations to agree. One of Audrey's major problems for the entire department was to institute a service Quality Management Program, and she wanted to start in the Business Services Group. Charles agreed with the idea.

Early the following Monday, Charles called the staff together for a meeting. He told them of Audrey's goal for instituting a Service Quality Management Program and that they were selected to begin it. He also told them that in order to move them forward, he was going to do two things, effective immediately:

- Raise their service quotas by 20 percent
- Submit anyone who failed to meet that quota to a formal disciplinary action

The specialists left the meeting without comment, although there was a lot of mumbling in the hallways as they walked back to their desks.

Over the next week or so, Charles noticed that they seemed to avoid him and were noticeably cooler to him when he was at hand. He had to make more of an effort to get information and ideas from them, and it seemed that the tone and tenor of the offices became more tense, hostile, and somber.

After two weeks, Charles reviewed the performance records of the specialists. Sure enough, Suzy Harris had not met her quota, and as promised, Charles issued a written reprimand to her. Suzy was speechless, though clearly angered by Charles, as he reviewed the reprimand with her.

It has been two days since that meeting. Since then, Suzy has filed a grievance in the Personnel Department against Charles. John Willis put in a request for a transfer, and Charles heard that Barbara Garrett is preparing to request a transfer. None of the employees in the Business Services Group now talk to him at all and simply pass along information in handwritten notes. He also has noticed how services to certain businesses have now slightly slipped.

He knows there is a major problem. As he sits at his desk at 5:00 p.m., in an empty office, waiting to make a call to one of the businesses that has complained, he wonders what went wrong and what he should do now.

CASE QUESTIONS

1. How should Charles have responded to his manager's interest in starting the Service Quality Management Program?

2. Describe the problem(s) facing Charles.

3. What should Charles do to respond to the problem(s)?

The Management Training Tool Kit: 35 Exercises to Prepare Managers for the Challenges They Face Every Day, ©2012 HRD Press.
Published by AMACOM Books, American Management Association, www.amanet.org.

Case Discussion:
Improving Performance in Business Services

Summary

Charles Thompson recently was appointed manager of the Business Services Department. Earlier in his career, he had worked as a specialist in this department for 18 months until he transferred to another department. When he moved back, he was reunited with a group he had previously worked with. This group, known officially as the Business Services Group, was experienced and its members were worked together effectively. Spurred by his new boss to improve service quality, Charles raised their quotas by 20 percent and threatened to put anyone who did not meet this quota on formal discipline. After two weeks, he did so to one employee. There is now a major morale problem and a grievance filed with the Personnel Department.

Answers to Case Questions

1. **How should Charles have responded to his manager's interest in starting the Service Quality Management Program?**

   Charles should have first clarified with the manager what her expectations were for this program, including deadlines, budget, outcomes, and learning activities. He should have reached some agreement with her about his authority to execute the program as he sees best and how they will communicate on the program's progress.

   The employees in the Business Services Group are in general a medium- to high-competence group. The recommended leadership style would be a participative one. This means that Charles should meet with the group's members and explain the situation, including all relevant background.

   At this meeting, Charles should solicit their input on identifying options for improving services. This may include seeking training resources, as well as providing service quality information. This first meeting would create a schedule for how the Business Services Group would plan and carry out this project. It would be possible to delegate specific assignments to each member of the group.

2. **Describe the problem(s) facing Charles.**

   Charles faces a serious morale problem that will likely escalate into lowered productivity, reduced communication, increased complaints, turnover, and conflict. This morale problem rests on a resentment and distrust of Charles's management practices.

3. **What should Charles do to respond to the problem(s)?**

   Charles used the wrong approach in seeking to produce change among his employee group. In effect, Charles created the reason for the problem by taking a directive approach when a more participative one was needed. Therefore, Charles should call a meeting with his staff to discuss the matter.

13

At the meeting, Charles should indicate that he made a mistake in his approach to the goals of improved service quality. Indeed, he should reaffirm his commitment to that process. However, he should take responsibility for the problem. Assuming that there were no complications in the grievance process, it would be appropriate to rescind the formal discipline on the employee in question.

It is likely that given the opportunity the employees may have repressed a level of anger about things in general and about Charles in particular. At this meeting, he should encourage them to raise that anger or any concerns so that he can make any changes needed to forestall future problems.

Either at this meeting or at one held in the near future, Charles should use a more participative process for instituting the Service Quality Management Program. At that point, he could pick up on the procedures discussed in the answer to Question 1.

Case 4 ✍

"Looney Tunes on Parade"

Part 1—*Getting Started on the Right (or Left?) Foot*

Background Information

Republic Insurance Company is a regional, all-purpose firm with offices in a three-state area. The central headquarters office houses the staff that plans and controls the field-office operations. Because the company is in such a competitive industry, sales play a very important role in Republic's efforts.

The group responsible for planning and controlling the sales effort of Republic's three-state field force is the Strategic Management Division. There are two main components of the Strategic Management Division:

1. The Accounting Department, which pays the bills and keeps track of the income.

2. The Plans Department, which does the marketing, product and price studies, profit forecasting, budget planning, and similar duties.

The organizational chart of this Strategic Management Division is shown below. It depicts the structure of the division and the leadership roles within that structure that have a bearing on this case. It also includes the names of the individuals who filled those leadership roles in June 1987, the time when the events in this case begin.

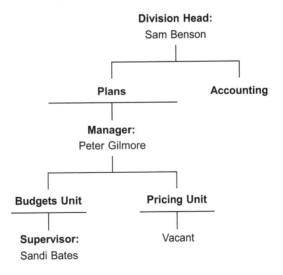

Strategic Management Division

Division Head:
Sam Benson

Plans — **Accounting**

Manager:
Peter Gilmore

Budgets Unit — **Pricing Unit**

Supervisor:
Sandi Bates

Vacant

15

The manager of the Plans Department is responsible for two units: Budgets and Pricing. Each unit has a supervisor who is responsible for the projects and tasks assigned to the unit. The Budgets Unit does long-term planning and evaluation of the profit-and-cost centers of Republic and coordinates the overall budget planning for the entire company. The Pricing Unit is responsible for keeping track of the competition's prices on insurance policies, company-wide profit forecasting, and other special studies about company products or costs. The Pricing Unit regularly provides these studies to other units and divisions within the company. These studies supply essential information to the managers of these other departments so that they can make their own business and budgeting plans.

In June 2007, the Strategic Management Division was headed by Sam Benson. Peter Gilmore, who had been with Republic for 10 years, managed the Plans Department's two units. The Budgets Unit was supervised by Sandi Bates, and the Pricing Unit's supervisory position was vacant.

In that same month, Peter Gilmore received a referral from Personnel for the open supervisor's position in the Pricing Unit. The job candidate's name was David Randle. David had a résumé that looked good (see the following page), and Peter managed to squeeze him in for a 20-minute interview between business meetings. The manager talked in general about the job and asked David about his résumé. He found David personable and easy to get along with, liked the candidate's background, and decided to offer him the job. He told Personnel to hire him and take care of the details.

David began work a week later, on July 1, 2007, as supervisor of the Pricing Unit. He had two cost analysts and a secretary reporting to him.

CASE QUESTIONS

1. Evaluate David Randle's résumé.

2. Evaluate the selection procedure used by Peter Gilmore.

3. Anticipate any effects of the selection procedure used by Peter on David's future performance.

The Management Training Tool Kit: 35 Exercises to Prepare Managers for the Challenges They Face Every Day, ©2012 HRD Press.
Published by AMACOM Books, American Management Association, www.amanet.org.

David Randle
5634 Watercrest Street
City, State 12345

Education:　State University
The Evening College Program

B.S. in Business
3.75 GPA, 3.8 in major
1997–2004

Personal:　Born: October 9, 1977
Married
Fluent in four languages:
Spanish, French, Italian, Portugese

Work History:　*Smith Stores*
January 2007–current

Cost Accountant: Supervises Cost Unit, profit-planning, budget coordination for the stores

Johnson Adhesives Manufacturing
February 2006–July 2006
Price Analyst: Developed and supervised computer records, inventory controls, payrolls

Safety Media Films
January 2003–February 2006
Price Analyst: Budget planning, international finance, financial planning

Bander Food Chains
November 2001–January 2003
Senior Bookkeeper: Price studies, computer records, supervision

Get Smart Book Publishers
February 2001–November 2001
Junior Bookkeeper: Payroll accounts, accounts receivable, payable, general ledger, audits

17

Approaching the Job of Supervisory Leadership

Peter Gilmore was a capable, energetic manager with the Republic Insurance Company. He began his career with Republic some 15 years ago, after graduating with an accounting degree from the night school program at City University. He was personable, well liked, and bright.

Peter worked hard and diligently, regularly putting in 10-hour days and work on the weekends. Because of his dedication, Peter had been rewarded with ever-increasing responsibilities and promotions. He was now serving effectively as the second in command in the Strategic Management Division.

Peter once summarized his supervisory philosophy and practice in this way: "You know, every time my boss gave me an assignment, I always worked as hard and as fast as I could to complete it perfectly and on time. I expect the same from my subordinates: If I give them something to do, I expect the same from them—it should be done correctly and on time. I can't take time to check up on them or see if they are doing it."

Peter's management practices were good to his word: He delegated projects easily and would expect them to get done. When he handed out an assignment, he didn't expect to have to deal with it again until the employee brought back the completed task within a reasonable time.

CASE QUESTIONS

1. For this type of supervisory leadership to work successfully, what kind of relationship must Peter Gilmore have with his subordinates? What characteristics must the employees possess?

2. What kind of problems, if any, might you expect from this kind of supervision?

3. What general kinds of supervisory actions should Peter be taking?

The Management Training Tool Kit: 35 Exercises to Prepare Managers for the Challenges They Face Every Day, ©2012 HRD Press.
Published by AMACOM Books, American Management Association, www.amanet.org.

Getting Things Under Control?

After a month or so of orientation and break-in, David Randle was regularly given assignments by his boss, Peter Gilmore. For example, one major assignment Peter gave to David involved proposed price changes in Republic's line of life insurance policies. These policies were a major income producer for Republic. Recent changes in the prices for similar products by the competition were beginning to put pressure on the profit margins of these products. Republic needed to maintain a strong and sound competitive posture in this sales area. This was a major, long-term study that would take about six or seven months to complete. During the period in which Peter was trying to hire a supervisor, he "babysat" the project. Once David was hired, Peter was more than happy to turn over the project to him.

Peter would give these studies and assignments to David and expect them to be done. Since many of these reports were prepared for other departments in the company, Peter did not necessarily see them once they were completed.

In addition, it turned out that Peter and David lived in the same part of town. Shortly after David was hired, he and Peter started commuting together to and from work. Peter felt that David had ample opportunity to talk with him if there were any problems or questions.

There had been a series of problems in the Pricing Unit, though, not long before David was hired. Work was not getting done properly through the unit, and at first no one knew why. Sam Benson (the head of the Strategic Management Division) finally determined that these problems had developed because requests for work were made directly to the Pricing Unit from other departments. Sam issued a standing order to the other divisions in Republic that the Pricing Unit would no longer take work requests directly from other departments. Instead, the requesting department had to submit its work order directly either to him or to Peter for initial approval.

David learned of this rule very quickly. When managers approached him for work assignments, David told them: "I'd really like to help. But you know the rule that Sam Benson laid down. You need to discuss the project with him."

During David's first six months on the job, everything seemed to be going fine. Peter would give David assignments and, not hearing anything to the contrary, would assume that the projects were being done. As far as Peter knew, all was well.

CASE QUESTIONS

1. Did Peter Gilmore need to establish any controls over the work of David Randle? Did Peter have adequate controls over the work?

2. What kind of control should Peter have established over the work of David and the Pricing Unit?

19

Case Discussion:

"Looney Tunes on Parade": Part 1—*Getting Started on the Right (or Left?) Foot*

Summary: Background Information

Peter Gilmore managed the Plans Department for Republic Insurance company. The Pricing Unit supervisor's job, one of the two supervisory positions that would report to Peter, became vacant. Peter spent about 20 minutes interviewing David Randle for the position, liked him, and told Personnel to hire him.

Answers to Case Questions

1. **Evaluate David Randle's résumé.**

   The résumé David provided indicates that he graduated from the Evening College Program of State University with a high grade point average (GPA) after attending classes for six years. He has a bachelor's degree in business and is multilingual. His work history shows a steady progression up the career ladder in the accounting field. He does appear to move from one job to the next fairly quickly, though. There is a six-month gap between his most recent job and the one held before it. Jobs held before 1981 are not reported, although he was in the Evening College Program during part of this period.

   In general, the résumé suggests he has a strong background.

2. **Evaluate the selection procedure used by Peter Gilmore.**

   Although there is limited detail, it does appear that Peter's selection procedure was off-the-cuff and informal. Peter apparently relied on David's résumé to define his technical background and paid more attention to how much he personally liked the candidate.

   Not mentioned in the case was the reliance on Personnel for follow-through. At Republic, Personnel contacted a private investigator to check out references and past employers. Personnel also requested new hirees to supply official copies of their college transcripts. If no transcripts were received after three months, Personnel ceased the request.

3. **Anticipate any effects of the selection procedure used by Peter on David's future performance.**

   Peter's casual approach to David's technical background and his reliance on personal chemistry are indicative of Peter's operating style. The lack of a rigorous selection process will have minimal impact on socializing David into the operations and culture of Republic Insurance.

Summary: Approaching the Job of Supervisory Leadership

Peter Gilmore was a dedicated, hard-working employee who had graduated from night school with an accounting degree. His diligence earned him progressive promotions through the company. He expected his employees to complete their assignments independently. Since he worked hard and took responsibility for his work, he expected his employees to do the same.

Answers to Case Questions

1. **For this type of supervisory leadership to work successfully, what kind of relationship must Peter Gilmore have with his subordinates? What characteristics must the employee possess?**

   For his style of leadership to work, Peter must have a very trusting relationship with his employees. He is relying on them to complete their work without his review. The employees must be like him: hard working, trained and capable, and willing to take responsibility.

2. **What kind of problems, if any, might you expect from this kind of supervision?**

   To the extent that employees may not be fully capable, there is a real potential for performance errors or delays. Problems such as these reverberate throughout an organization, affecting the employees and the quality of service they provide, and generating stress and conflict. These problems could reach the point of turnover or termination.

   To the extent that the employee is not trustworthy, Peter's entire style of managing is compromised, putting stress on him and lowering the productivity of others.

3. **What general kinds of supervisory actions should Peter be taking?**

   There are two main actions Peter should be taking at this stage in managing David Randle. First, he should be planning and completing an orientation period for David. Second, he should be scheduling regular review meetings with David to examine the quality of the work being performed to guide David in new assignments.

Summary: Getting Things Under Control?

During David Randle's first six months on the job, he appeared to settle well. Peter Gilmore would give him assignments and expect them to be done. Since Peter and David commuted to work together, Peter assumed they had ample opportunity to discuss any problems. Not hearing of any problems, Peter figured all was going well.

Answers to Case Questions

1. **Did Peter Gilmore need to establish any controls over the work of David Randle? Did Peter have adequate controls over the work?**

   Yes, Peter did need controls, but he apparently did not have them. Peter needed some way to determine on a regular basis what David was doing and how well it was being done. He did not have such a procedure in place, however.

2. **What kind of control should Peter have established over the work of David and the Pricing Unit?**

   In this kind of situation, Peter could have used two different control procedures. First, following an MBO-type approach, he should have kept a log of all the projects assigned to David. Then, in regular sessions (perhaps weekly at first), he should have gotten updates from David on the progress of each. At the start, he should have reviewed the actual products (reports, memos, and the like).

   Second, Peter should use some method to contact the recipients of these reports to assess their satisfaction with the quality of reports received.

Case 5 ✍

"Looney Tunes on Parade"
Part 2—*Kicking into Gear*

Background Information

Peter Gilmore, manager, hired David Randle in July 2007 to supervise the Pricing Unit of Republic Insurance Corporation's Strategic Management Division. The Pricing Unit conducted important studies about the competitive posture of Republic's various policy products. Once David was hired, Peter delegated assignments to David often and easily. Peter expected these assignments to be completed and returned on a timely basis, although he did not check on progress during the interim.

Flares in the Night

In December 2007, six months after he was hired, things still seemed to be going smoothly for the new supervisor of the Pricing Unit, David Randle—at least on the surface. Nonetheless, Peter Gilmore was feeling uneasy. As he later put it: "It was nothing I could put my finger on exactly. I just didn't feel comfortable trusting him." In fact, Peter had been receiving some information about David that was giving him some cause for concern.

One source of this information was supervisor Sandi Bates. Sandi, David Randle's counterpart in the Budgets Unit, also reported to Peter Gilmore. It became clear not long after David was hired that he and Sandi simply did not get along. Peter was not too concerned, feeling the problem was just a difference in personalities. There were periodic flashes of anger and occasional back-biting. Finally, in January, Peter lost his patience and told the two of them: "I don't want this fighting anymore. You two work out your differences and get this squabbling resolved."

In early March, Sandi asked to see Peter privately. She told him that she had tried to resolve these problems, but with little success. She also told him that David was "screwing up" some of the projects Peter had given him. Peter asked David about these "screw-ups" a few days later. David conceded that he had been having some difficulties because of family problems. Peter took him at his word, but still felt uneasy.

In mid-March, a second matter of concern developed. The source of this concern was David's new sideline venture: a mail-order supply business that he had started with his brother-in-law in February. David would occasionally solicit other employees in the headquarters' office for orders. Peter was amused at first, but in mid-March, employees started calling his office to complain that David was not filling their orders.

By April, 10 months after David had started with Republic, Peter was definitely bothered by David. He wondered to himself: "What's going on here? Is Randle too busy or is he incompetent, or what? Something just isn't right."

The Management Training Tool Kit: 35 Exercises to Prepare Managers for the Challenges They Face Every Day, ©2012 HRD Press.
Published by AMACOM Books, American Management Association, www.amanet.org.

To deal with this concern, he talked with David and asked the supervisor to complete a long self-assessment form he had picked up at a conference a few years earlier. It contained a list of skills for accountants in project management. The person completing the assessment rated his or her current skill levels on a scale of 1 to 7. Peter wanted David to identify any job performance weaknesses he might have and to start improving them.

David filled out the form and told Peter that the assessment was very helpful and that he could see performance areas he needed to improve immediately. Sure enough, Peter seemed to notice some improvement in David's work during the next few weeks.

CASE QUESTIONS

1. What was happening at this point?

2. What should Peter Gilmore do at this point?

The Management Training Tool Kit: 35 Exercises to Prepare Managers for the Challenges They Face Every Day, ©2012 HRD Press.
Published by AMACOM Books, American Management Association, www.amanet.org.

Changing the Guard

Sam Benson had been head of the Strategic Management Division at Republic Insurance for nearly six years. He served well in this capacity, capping a 30-year career with Republic by retiring in April 2008.

Sam was replaced by Henry Carpenter, 41. Henry had been with Republic for almost three years, serving as chief information management officer. Henry moved into Sam Benson's office during David Randle's eleventh month with Republic in May.

It seemed to Peter Gilmore that from that day forward, David spent a lot of time with Henry. He could often be found in Henry's office, no matter what time of day it was. They would have lunch together or go out for drinks after work. Beyond these social contacts, Henry began assigning projects directly to David. Often these assignments were made without Peter even knowing about it. Peter, who suspected as much, was too busy to give the matter serious thought. "What the heck," he told himself. "Let Henry work with him, too."

Not long after, though, when David was on vacation, an incident occurred that convinced Peter that his vague intuitions about something not being right with David were well founded. Sometime earlier in April, David had conducted a performance evaluation of Betty Moore, one of the cost analysts in David's Pricing Unit. During the evaluation, David promised to make Betty a supervisor and arrange for her to receive a 20 percent salary increase. (In fact, Republic had a policy that the maximum salary adjustment to which anyone was entitled during a six-month period was 14 percent.) By May, when Betty saw no change in her salary, she met with Peter privately. Betty had worked with Peter for over four years.

Betty began: "You know, David did my performance appraisal two months ago, and he promised me a supervisory promotion and a 20 percent salary increase. But I haven't received either yet. Is there something wrong?"

Peter was surprised. "David promised what?" he asked in astonishment. He was very aware of the firm's policy on salary increases and knew that David was also aware of them.

Betty repeated her comments. As Peter listened to Betty's explanation, his anger rose. When Betty finished, he called Bill Schmidt to join them. Bill was Betty's colleague and the other cost analyst that David supervised.

Peter said, "Bill, Betty has been telling me some things that I find very distressing about David's management practices. Tell me what's going on there."

He got an earful. The analysts told him that David never gave them any work to do on any kind of regular basis. They did not know what he did with the assignments he received from Peter or Henry, but every so often, David would give them a real rush job on a big project and then pressure them until it was finished. When David finally received their report, he would put his name on it and pass it along.

Peter now became very angry. He thanked Betty and Bill for their honesty. As soon as they left, he walked into Henry's office and made three points: "One, I don't trust David, and I may want to fire him. Two, I think you and David are getting way too close. And three, in the future, tell me if you make any assignments directly to David." Peter's irritation was obvious, and Henry patiently waited for him to calm down. Peter then told Henry what he just learned from Betty and Bill.

25

The Management Training Tool Kit: 35 Exercises to Prepare Managers for the Challenges They Face Every Day, ©2012 HRD Press.
Published by AMACOM Books, American Management Association, www.amanet.org.

After returning to his office, Peter phoned David at his home. David's wife answered the call and told him that David was not available.

Peter said pointedly: "Tell David that we will not be commuting to work anymore together."

Sensing something in Peter's tone, Mrs. Randle started talking about all the family problems David was having. Peter ended the conversation as quickly as possible.

David was now approaching his first year's anniversary with Republic Insurance, and his performance appraisal was due. When he returned from vacation the following week, the evaluation was waiting (see the next page for Peter's appraisal of David). During the discussion, Peter told David that there had better be improvement in his performance—or else.

Again, David seemed to make a recovery. He came into work early, worked hard, stayed busy, was quiet, and stayed late.

But Peter was watching him closely now.

CASE QUESTIONS

1. What are the problems at this point?

2. Evaluate how well Peter Gilmore is handling these problems.

3. Recommend how Peter should deal with the problems.

4. Evaluate Peter's performance appraisal of David.

The Management Training Tool Kit: 35 Exercises to Prepare Managers for the Challenges They Face Every Day, ©2012 HRD Press.
Published by AMACOM Books, American Management Association, www.amanet.org.

Republic Insurance

Employee Evaluation

Employee: David Randle **Date:** June 2008
Position: Supervisor, Pricing Unit
Manager: Peter Gilmore

1. Describe the employee's overall performance.

   David has the skills to become one of the top performers of this division. However, during the past year, he has done only a satisfactory job.

2. Describe the employee's work habits and accomplishments.

   David usually finishes his work on time. He has a strong tendency to let projects slide and then try to get them done at the last minute.

3. Future skills development plans.

   Improve knowledge of insurance and accounting. Develop career plan.

David Randle   Peter Gilmore

_____   _____

The Management Training Tool Kit: 35 Exercises to Prepare Managers for the Challenges They Face Every Day, ©2012 HRD Press.
Published by AMACOM Books, American Management Association, www.amanet.org.

Case Discussion:
"Looney Tunes on Parade": Part 2—*Kicking into Gear*

Summary: Flares in the Night

As manager, Peter Gilmore readily delegated assignments to his new Pricing Unit manager, David Randle. Peter expected David to finish the projects on his own and did not check up on David's progress. After six months, though, Peter began to receive signals that all was not well. For example, David's counterpart supervisor, Sandi Bates, told Peter that David has been "screwing up" some assignments. Peter also began to get complaints from employees about David not filling personal orders for merchandise placed through his sideline mail-order business. Peter had David complete a self-assessment of his skills, and the situation seemed to improve.

Answers to Case Questions

1. **What was happening at this point?**

   By now, David should have become sufficiently oriented to performing his tasks adequately. However, Peter does not know how well David has been doing his work because he has not asked. David and his peer supervisor have some kind of "personality" conflict. Further, David is conducting a personal business venture on company time and premises. This can be a problem if the company has a no solicitation policy. In general, Peter has a general sense of unease with David. Peter has David complete a self-assessment exercise. However, this exercise is not really relevant to what should be the key issue: David's job performance.

2. **What should Peter Gilmore do at this point?**

   Peter should do several things. First, he should instruct David to cease and desist any and all private business solicitation. Second, he should meet with Sandi Bates to listen more adequately and fully to her reports on David. He may need to spend more time managing the Bates and David relationship to reduce difficulties. This could be done through such steps as creating common goals for both, more clearly defining respective job duties, and/or looking for ways to resolve any operating conflicts. Finally, Peter should ask David to provide a full and complete accounting of where he stands on all the projects he has been assigned. At this point, Peter does not know what David has done. David is out of Peter's control.

28

Summary: Changing the Guard

When the head of the Strategic Management Division retired, he was replaced by Henry Carpenter, who had been managing another division in the company. David Randle began fraternizing with Henry Carpenter almost as soon as Henry moved in. Peter Gilmore noticed how quickly David and Henry had become friends. Although he had a vague feeling that something was not quite right about David, he did not become alarmed about the supervisor until one of David's employees inquired about the status of her performance increase and promotion, which David had promised her some time ago.

Upon investigating the matter further with a second employee, Peter learned that David seldom supervised employees, but would occasionally pressure them into completing an assignment that he would later put his name on. After he discovered this, Peter alerted Henry, then phoned David, who was home on vacation. He told David's wife that they would not be commuting together to work anymore. David's wife mentioned that she and her husband were having family problems lately. Next, Peter prepared an evaluation of David to coincide with the supervisor's first anniversary with the company.

Answers to Case Questions

1. **What are the problems at this point?**

   The immediate problems are several. One is that Peter now trusts David very little. A second is that David has insinuated himself into a friendly relationship with Peter's boss. Third, David has acted inappropriately with his employees, creating morale and production problems. The deeper, latent problem concerns the extent to which David has been performing his job tasks effectively. Peter cannot answer this question.

2. **Evaluate how well Peter Gilmore is handling these problems.**

   In some ways, Peter is acting appropriately. For example, he directly investigated David's supervision once he was tipped off by a disgruntled employee. It is not clear in the case what action he took to resolve that employee's problem, although he should have initiated some action. He also acted well in alerting his boss to a problem and implying that Henry should distance himself from David. He also acted well in severing their relationship as commuters.

   However, Peter still does not know how well David has been doing his job. He has not asked for a follow-up. Furthermore, Peter should have counseled David on his supervisory practices. In some contexts, David's plagiarism of employee work would be considered unethical and worthy of disciplinary action. Finally, David's evaluation is rather weak and superficial.

3. **Recommend how Peter should deal with the problems.**

   Peter should ask for a full and complete accounting of the status of all projects assigned to David. He should counsel David about his supervision practices and make sure that the problem with David's employee is resolved as effectively as possible. He also should determine whether disciplinary action is warranted for David's plagiarism. The performance appraisal should be more clear and forceful.

4. Evaluate Peter's performance appraisal of David.

Peter's evaluation of David was insufficient. He needs to provide more detail of specific areas of performance. He should note past instances of performance problems (sideline business activities, supervisory practices). He should state that David must improve significantly or termination may be necessary.

Case 6 ✍

"Looney Tunes on Parade":
Part 3—*A Time for Action*

Background Information

Just over a year after Peter Gilmore hired David Randle to supervise the Pricing Unit Department of Republic Insurance's Strategic Management Division, Peter was faced with a number of problems. The initial period of smooth sailing had deteriorated, as revelations about David's questionable conduct had surfaced. In response to these revelations, Peter completed an appraisal of David's job performance, warning him that he needed to make improvements in this area. Peter was now watching David closely.

Peter's new "get-tough" supervisory style yielded a number of results. It was now early July 2008, and the Life Insurance Line Price Study for which David was responsible was a few months overdue. The head of the Customer Services Division had called Peter last week to ask him where it was. This time, Peter knew to ask David for it.

David said it would be ready the next day and, sure enough, the following morning it was on Peter's desk. At an early-morning coffee break, Peter asked Betty Moore if any of the cost analysts had prepared this report. Betty replied, "No, David did it all himself late yesterday afternoon."

Peter started to read the report, and one thing immediately became apparent: the numbers and calculations did not seem correct. And there was something else that wasn't right about the report. At first, he just couldn't figure out what it was; then, he remembered. He went to his bookcase, pulled out the February 1986 issue of *Life Insurance Digest,* and there it was: David Randle's report—or rather, the *Digest* article that David had copied and used for his report.

Peter talked with Henry Carpenter that afternoon, and both agreed that David must go. The next morning, David was sitting in front of Henry and Peter in Peter's office.

Henry began: "David, a week ago when we discussed this price change study, the figures you gave me were quite different from the figures in this report. What the heck is going on?" Henry was angry, and his tone was harsh.

David shifted in his chair. "Well, er, the figures I gave you were still tentative. They were, ah, still estimates." David did not look at either of them and fidgeted slightly in his seat.

Henry continued: "The Knilson Actuarial Count equation is a basic formula for computing the real market pricing for our life insurance policies. I want to see you do it, here, now!"

David was now visibly shaken and said lamely: "Well, Hank, as you know, I'll need my work papers. Let me go back to my desk, I don't want to take your time…maybe there is a specific error I made that—"

31

Henry cut him off: "No sir, here and now. We'll supply you with the information. Use this pen and pad of paper." Henry pushed the items toward him.

David picked up the pen and began writing down some numbers. After a minute, he looked up and started to explain his results.

Peter interrupted him: "David, you don't know what you're doing. You've got two of the basic parameters confused, and you just don't know what the heck you're doing… You copied this article virtually verbatim from the *Life Insurance Digest*, didn't you?" Peter pushed the article across the desk, in front of David.

David was stunned.

Peter said, "Let's go to Personnel, David. You are no longer an employee of Republic Insurance."

At 10:30 a.m., David Randle walked to the street in front of the Republic Insurance Company, and by 10:45 a.m. he was no longer in sight.

CASE QUESTIONS

1. Evaluate the termination procedure used.

2. Are there any legal considerations in releasing David Randle in this manner? Are there any legal grounds for prosecuting David?

3. What should Peter do now with his staff?

The Management Training Tool Kit: 35 Exercises to Prepare Managers for the Challenges They Face Every Day, ©2012 HRD Press.
Published by AMACOM Books, American Management Association, www.amanet.org.

Postmortems

Later that morning, after Peter told his staff that David was fired, he and Betty Moore cleaned out David's desk and files. When they were finished, they had assembled a pile of papers over a foot high. These papers were all the projects and assignments Peter had given David over the past year. They had been thrown in drawers, in cabinets, wherever, and had not been touched.

About a week later, Peter received a rather alarming report from another Republic employee. This employee had been to David's house earlier in the day to pick up a mail-order shipment. While she was there, David made a comment that was a threat on Peter's life. Peter told Henry, and Henry called David's house, demanding an explanation. Henry threatened to call the police. David laughed and said he was only joking.

The circumstances surrounding David's termination alerted the Personnel Department, which proceeded to investigate what had happened more carefully. Upon reviewing their files of David Randle, they found out two rather disturbing facts. First, David had been fired from every job he had held as an adult. This fact was hinted at in the standard background check conducted by a private investigator. At the time the report was submitted, the references had been indecisive (see the report on the next page). Second, it was also discovered that, contrary to the information on his résumé, David had attended State University for only one year and did not have a bachelor's degree.

When Peter learned of these last tidbits, he just smiled, shook his head, and said: "Looney tunes on parade."

33

ACME PERSONNEL INVESTIGATIONS

Under Contract 2007–482 to
Republic Insurance

CONFIDENTIAL

Date _____

Applicant: David Randle

Smith Stores: 1/2007 to date

Payroll clerk verifies applicant was employed from January to June as a Cost Accountant. SSN verified.

Johnson Adhesives Manufacturing: 2/2006 to 7/2006

Personnel Clerk verifies applicant employed as Price Analyst from February 1986 through July 1986. SSN verified. Applicant was laid off due to cost cutting.

Safety Media Films: 1/2003 to 2/2006

No listing found for the above place of business. Apparently it is out of business.

Bander Food Chains: 11/2001 to 1/2003

Account Manager verified that applicant was employed from November 1981 to December 9, 1983, as a Senior Bookkeeper. Apparently, his work was satisfactory as nothing in the file is derogatory. It was noted that he was discharged. However, this was probably due to a change in supervisors at that time.

Get Smart Book Publishers: 2/2001 to 11/2001

Clerk verified that applicant was Junior Bookkeeper from February 2001 through November 2001. This was all the information she could give over the telephone.

The Management Training Tool Kit: 35 Exercises to Prepare Managers for the Challenges They Face Every Day, ©2012 HRD Press.
Published by AMACOM Books, American Management Association, www.amanet.org.

Case Discussion:
"Looney Tunes on Parade" Part 3—*A Time for Action*

Summary: Background Information

Over the course of a year's time, Peter Gilmore had become increasingly distrustful of David Randle, the man he had hired to supervise the Pricing Unit group of the department he managed. Peter believed that employees should carry out the assignments they were given without a manager having to check up on them. After six months, Peter began to learn that there were certain peculiarities in how David worked, such as running a sideline business in the workplace and plagiarizing employee work. He now began to watch David closely. He gave David an assignment only to discover that the report David later submitted on that assignment had been copied from a professional publication. In response to this discovery, Peter and his boss, Henry Carpenter, met with David the following day and instructed him to complete a standard calculation. David could not do it and was terminated for poor performance.

Answers to Case Questions

1. **Evaluate the termination procedure used.**

   While somewhat unorthodox, the method used was perfectly legal and very acceptable. They could have fired him solely on the grounds of submitting false information, but taking this additional step confirms their belief and further supports their rationale for termination: David is not qualified to retain his position. In taking this additional step and given the absence of specific job performance information, they know they are fully justified in deciding to release David from the company.

2. **Are there any legal considerations in releasing David Randle in this manner? Are there any legal grounds for prosecuting David?**

   One potential problem might be the way the test was administered—under stressful and threatening conditions. If David wanted to push the matter, he could contend that he knew how to answer the problem but was inhibited from doing so by the way it was presented to him. In itself, this is a valid point; however, given the context of the entire matter, it would have secondary significance.

   At this point, based upon what is known, there are no grounds for prosecuting David Randle. That is, there is no evidence of fraud or embezzlement known at this stage.

3. **What should Peter Gilmore do now with his staff?**

   Peter Gilmore should meet with the staff to explain that David has been released and to plan for interim steps. There could be a potential libel issue here if Peter explains the reason for David's termination in ways that impugn David's character. Truthful statements, though, are defensible, such as "David was released because he copied a report without attribution." In general, though, Peter should focus more on what to do next rather than on David. Peter should instruct his employees that any calls or inquiries regarding David Randle should be forwarded to either him or to Personnel. Peter should, however, order an audit of David's budget and related matters as a precaution.

Summary: Postmortems

There were several aftereffects of the David Randle termination. First, Peter Gilmore discovered an enormous pile of work that David had not completed. Second, and most significant, it was determined that David was a fraud. He did not have a college degree, and he had been fired from every previous job he had. The background check obtained at the time of David's hire had been suggestive but inconclusive.

Case 7 ✍️

Mary Corey

Background Information

Mary Corey recently completed her fourth year with Statewide Services Corporation. In her position as customer support specialist, she consistently received high performance evaluations—until recently. Indeed, her most recent evaluation, completed three weeks ago, rated her as "less than satisfactory." Her supervisor, Helen Rowe, wondered why this previously strong employee had fallen so quickly.

Helen had just returned from a meeting with her boss, Betty Allen, when again the subject of Mary came up. Betty suggested that Helen look through Mary's past work records to try to find some clues about what happened and what they should do now.

Helen closed the door to her office, sat at her desk, and pulled Mary's personnel folder from her desk drawer. As she flipped through the materials in the folder, Mary's story came into better focus:

> About six months ago, around Christmastime, Mary started taking longer lunch breaks. Given the cramped quarters in which Helen's Customer Support Department worked and the demanding routines they had to follow, it was easy to notice Mary stretching her regular lunch period by 10 or 15 minutes. Once she even stretched it for a full 25 minutes. Since it was the holiday season, Helen took no specific action. However, her occasional remarks reminding Mary of the lunch break schedules would produce an uncharacteristically evasive, defensive response from Mary. On at least two occasions, she nodded off to sleep at her desk after returning from lunch.

> In January and February, she was 10 to 20 minutes late for work on six different days and called in sick on four other days. It was during this time that Mary's dealings with her coworkers deteriorated. Normally quiet yet sociable, Mary became increasingly short-tempered and given to periodic outbursts of anger and belligerence. Since Mary, 36, was a single mother of two teenage girls, almost everyone in the office assumed there was something going on at home.

> On February 23rd, though, things took a disturbing turn. Mary left for lunch at her usual time, but did not return. She called in three hours later to say she had gone home because she had suddenly become ill. Her speech seemed slurred, somehow not quite right. She returned to work two days later, with a doctor's note explaining she had been sick with a stomach flu.

> Nonetheless, the pattern of lateness continued. Two weeks later, Helen gave Mary her first written disciplinary notice regarding her attendance and punctuality. During the discussion, Mary confessed to Helen: "I know I've

37

been a little different recently. I'm just having some problems at home with my children." She didn't elaborate, and Helen didn't probe.

For the next few weeks, Mary was on time every day and rarely left her desk during working hours. Her level of performance improved, as did her interaction with coworkers.

By April, however, Helen noticed Mary slipping back into her negative habits of lateness and irritability. Helen began to notice something else in Mary's after-lunch behavior: She seemed to have real difficulty completing her work, making decisions, and solving problems. On one occasion, there was a big argument between her and several coworkers. Mary went home, claiming she was "too upset to work." She continued coming in late to work and was absent on two successive Mondays. However, after each absence, she produced a doctor's excuse.

In early May, Helen issued a second written warning, this one concerning not only Mary's punctuality and attendance, but also her deteriorating work performance. At this time, Helen made it clear that Mary's continued employment was on the line: "I don't know what's going on, but you're in danger of losing your job. I've tried to be understanding, but I'm losing my patience. You need to get straightened up and soon, or I'll have no choice but to let you go."

During the following weeks, Mary again improved her productivity and performance. She was obviously concerned about losing her job. By mid-July, it was time for her formal performance evaluation. Although her evaluation was "less than satisfactory," Helen did note that there had been some improvement in all areas recently.

Then, last week, the bottom fell out. On July 23rd, Mary returned from lunch 45 minutes late, glassy-eyed and weaving slightly, fumbling with things and smelling strongly of peppermint. She sat at her desk for a full 20 minutes, rummaging through drawers, moving paper, nodding, spilling things, and creating quite a distraction among the other employees.

Helen came to her desk: "Mary, what's the matter here? Something's wrong, and you don't seem able to work at all. Are you ill? Can you work? Are you drunk? Tell me right now!"

Mary slowly looked up, taking a while to focus on Helen. After what seemed like a minute or so, during which time she appeared to be again listening to Helen's remarks, Mary burst into tears. She grabbed her purse, pushed and stumbled past Helen, and left.

The next day, one of Mary's children called in, saying Mary couldn't work because she was "in bed sick." Helen checked and Mary had only three remaining days of accrued sick leave available to her.

The Management Training Tool Kit: 35 Exercises to Prepare Managers for the Challenges They Face Every Day, ©2012 HRD Press.
Published by AMACOM Books, American Management Association, www.amanet.org.

Mary did not return to work until today. She went to the ladies room for an hour. When she emerged, she went into Helen's office and asked for an immediate transfer to some other department "where the pressure isn't so great." She seemed very agitated and would not look Helen in the eye. Helen told her to return to her desk and pick up on her work as well as she could until Helen could look into things more closely.

It was then that Helen met with her boss, Betty Alden. They were trying to decide what to do.

In thinking about where things stood now, Helen knew that Mary's presence in the unit was becoming a source of contention and disgruntlement. Everyone knew that she had some kind of problem, and most people thought it was due to drugs or alcohol, or both, although no one had ever personally seen her use or abuse either. Since her work was now so erratic, the other employees in the unit had to regularly back up her work by either finishing it or correcting it. She seemed to have no remorse about her conduct and could not presently be counted on to make an effort to correct it.

Helen wanted to fire her. As she explained to Betty: "When she's here, she fights with everyone, and I'm never sure when she's coming to work or how long she'll stay. She's hopeless. I hate to do this, but she has screwed up just too much."

Betty, as unit manager, could see that a previously valued and productive member of her department had for some reason, fallen well below accepted work standards. Both Betty and Helen believed there must be some serious, extenuating circumstances affecting Mary, although they didn't know for certain what it was. Betty was concerned whether there could be any legal problems in firing someone in this condition. Betty reminded Helen that the company did have an Employee Assistance Program (EAP) and wondered whether they should try to involve Mary in the EAP before taking further action.

CASE QUESTIONS

1. Can Helen terminate Mary without running into legal problems?

2. What should Helen do now regarding the Employee Assistance Program? Simulate how you would make a referral to the EAP if you were Helen.

3. Should Helen have acted sooner? If so, how?

The Management Training Tool Kit: 35 Exercises to Prepare Managers for the Challenges They Face Every Day, ©2012 HRD Press.
Published by AMACOM Books, American Management Association, www.amanet.org.

Case Discussion:
Mary Corey

Summary

Helen Rowe supervised the Customer Support Department for Statewide Services Corporation. Over the past six months, one of Helen's top performers, Mary Corey, had fallen into a situation of poor performance. In looking through her personnel folder, Helen reconstructed the history of Mary's decline, which follows.

About six months ago, at Christmastime, Mary began taking longer lunch breaks. When Helen made some comments, Mary was uncharacteristically defensive. Helen noticed that Mary fell asleep at her desk on two occasions. Then, beginning in January, Mary occasionally came into work 10 to 20 minutes late or did not come in at all because she was sick. During this period, Mary was increasingly short tempered with her coworkers. Her coworkers thought that Mary, a single mother of two teenage girls, might be having some problems at home.

In late February, Mary did not return from lunch one day. She called three hours later, claiming to have become ill. Her voice sounded slurred. She returned two days later with a doctor's note explaining she had a stomach flu. After repeated lateness, Helen issued Mary a formal disciplinary notice, and her attendance improved.

By April, Mary was slipping back to lateness and irritability. But now Mary also seemed to have problems completing her work after returning from lunch. In early May, Helen issued a second notice, indicating that this time Mary's job was on the line. Mary's performance improved again. However, she was given a less than satisfactory evaluation on her performance evaluation shortly thereafter.

Last week, after returning to work 45 minutes late and smelling strongly of peppermint, she created quite a commotion while trying to settle into her work. Helen confronted Mary, at which point Mary burst into tears and ran from the office. The next day, one of Mary's children called saying Mary was sick.

When Mary returned to work today, she asked for a transfer to an area with less pressure. Helen, concerned about the impact Mary was having on the Customer Support Department, wanted to fire her. The company did have an Employee Assistance Program (EAP).

Answers to Case Questions

1. Can Helen terminate Mary without running into legal problems?

Mary has been demonstrating behaviors that point to alcohol and/or drug abuse. One drawback for Helen is that she does not know whether it is alcohol, drugs, or a combination of both that is at the root of Mary's problem. Under the Americans with Disabilities Act, current illegal drug use is not protected. Thus, if Mary's problem is due exclusively to illegal drug use, Mary would have no protections under the law and could be terminated with minimal concern.

Alcohol abuse, on the other hand, is protected under the Rehabilitation Act of 1973: employees with an alcohol abuse problem cannot be discriminated against in employment based on this disability as long as they can perform their job duties safely and effectively. Employees with this condition, though, can be held to the same standards of performance as other employees.

To the extent that Mary's problem might be alcohol based, then, there could be some legal ramifications to firing her. However, given her erratic performance, a strong case could be made that she cannot perform her job effectively at the standards established.

A larger question, though, is whether termination is the best course of action here. In this case, Mary Corey was a very competent employee until recently, when things obviously went wrong. What kind of responsibility does an employer have for an employee, especially a good employee with a long history with the company? Unfortunately, Helen has dragged her feet in this matter and reduced her flexibility in acting (see Question 3). Still, it might be prudent to refer Mary to the Employee Assistance Program (EAP) that is available through Statewide Services.

2. What should Helen do now regarding the Employee Assistance Program? Simulate how you would make a referral to the EAP if you were Helen.

Helen should note Mary's behavior problems and indicate that Mary is in immediate jeopardy of losing her job. Helen should indicate that a transfer is out of the question because of Mary's poor performance recently. Helen could then suggest that the only option to immediate termination would be Mary's participation in the Employee Assistance Program.

Helen should explain that the EAP would report to her on Mary's attendance but that the subjects discussed would be confidential. Helen could encourage Mary's participation and indicate that she is concerned about Mary's well-being and would hate to lose an employee who had performed well. Helen should also make it clear that Mary will be held to the same standards as everyone else and that the next instance of violating a standard will result in Mary's immediate termination.

At this point, it could be a very good idea to give Mary the rest of the day off, with pay, so that she can make up her mind about what she wants to do.

Under this nonpunitive disciplinary procedure, Mary would be expected to decide what she wants to do. The next morning, she is to report directly to Helen's office with her decision. That decision would be either to

- resign because she cannot agree to meet the established standards of performance; or
- agree to meet the standards of the job, which may include participating in the EAP.

However, the stricture about no further violations of standards still applies.

3. Should Helen have acted sooner? If so, how?

Yes. It was clear early on that Mary was under the influence of a harmful and debilitating abusive substance(s). Helen should have referred Mary to the Employee Assistance Program much sooner.

Case 8 ✍

Shipping and Receiving

Background Information

Midge Watson had been working in the Bookkeeping Department of the Best Fits Sporting Goods Manufacturing Company for the four years since she graduated from high school. She was bright, attractive, and popular, and had done well in the company, as her recent promotion to senior bookkeeper proved.

One of her new job responsibilities required Midge to go to the warehouse once a week to check on and verify various inventory and shipment information. This meant that she often worked for three or four hours at a time in the Shipping Office. In order to reduce the noise from the operations around it, the office was completely walled in. On these trips to Shipping, Midge worked closely with the shipping clerk, Susan Adams. Susan, a veteran employee of ten years with Best Fit, was divorced. Susan maintained all the shipping and inventory information as it was processed.

Since Midge had never before worked in an actual manufacturing and warehouse operation, she was nervous at first. However, she was very relieved to find that Susan was very nice and helpful. Midge found Susan easy to talk to because Susan seemed so interested in what Midge was thinking and doing.

During her fourth visit to the warehouse, Midge and Susan were talking as usual about the week's shipping activity. As they were talking, Susan casually walked to Midge's side of the desk and sat on the edge of the desk right next to Midge.

Midge tried not to feel uncomfortable with Susan so close. At a break in the discussion, Susan looked at Midge very seriously and asked her: "Do you like to go dancing?"

Midge, a little surprised by the question, replied evenly: "Well, I like to, but I have a difficult time getting my boyfriend to go. He'd just as soon go drin—"

Susan interrupted: "I wasn't talking about your boyfriend. Would you like to go dancing with me?"

Midge, not sure what Susan was getting at, laughed and said: "Well, sure, maybe sometime.…" Her voice trailed off. She was trying to be polite but did not really want to commit herself.

Midge picked up a file and brought their discussion back to shipping information. She finished her work, then returned to her department. She was uneasy about Susan's behavior and invitation.

When she returned to her desk, Midge's supervisor, Mike Polski, noticed that she seemed to be distracted and asked if everything was okay. Midge explained what had just occurred and wondered if Susan had some ulterior motive for asking her to go dancing.

Mike, not sensing a problem, shrugged off what happened. "I wouldn't give it much thought, he advised Midge. You're probably reading something into Susan's comments. Don't be concerned."

43

The Management Training Tool Kit: 35 Exercises to Prepare Managers for the Challenges They Face Every Day, ©2012 HRD Press.
Published by AMACOM Books, American Management Association, www.amanet.org.

Next week, at her regular time, Midge returned to the warehouse. As she walked into the Shipping Office and closed the door, Susan jumped up from her chair and walked briskly over to Midge, smiling. She put her arms around Midge and hugged her tightly. After stroking Midge's back and patting her on the rear-end, she looked into Midge's eyes and told her: "Midge, I really missed you. I'm glad you're back."

Midge was completely startled, shocked, and afraid. She wiggled free and began to cry. Dropping the file she was carrying, she ran from the office back to her department. By the time Midge arrived, she had calmed down to some degree, but was still upset as she entered Mike Polski's office to describe what just happened.

CASE QUESTIONS

1. Is this a case of sexual harassment?

2. Does the company have a responsibility and/or liability?

3. What should the supervisor do now?

The Management Training Tool Kit: 35 Exercises to Prepare Managers for the Challenges They Face Every Day, ©2012 HRD Press.
Published by AMACOM Books, American Management Association, www.amanet.org.

Case Discussion:
Shipping and Receiving

Summary

Midge Watson was a young, attractive senior bookkeeping clerk for a manufacturer of sports clothes. In this capacity, Midge was required to go to the Shipping Office in the warehouse every week to verify inventory records. The Shipping Office was completely enclosed and private. Whenever she went there, Midge would work closely with Susan Adams, the shipping clerk. They worked well together, and Midge had no reason to anticipate any problems from Susan. Nonetheless, during one meeting, Susan sat very close to Midge and asked her if she wanted to go out dancing together. Midge left shortly thereafter and informed her boss, Mike Polski, about what had happened. He shrugged off her comments.

When Midge arrived at the Shipping Office the following week, Susan rushed over to her, hugged her tightly, stroked her back, and patted her rear-end, and told Midge how much she had missed her. Midge was shocked and afraid. She broke free of Susan and ran back to her department, crying. She told Mike Polski what had happened.

Answers to Case Questions

1. **Is this a case of sexual harassment?**

   Yes. Sexual harassment is unwanted sexual advances or requests for sexual favors or any conduct of a sexual nature that creates a hostile, intimidating, or offensive work environment. Such advances do not need to come only from a member of the opposite sex.

   Based on Midge's reactions and statements, it is clear that she did not welcome Susan's actions; she also finds those actions offensive.

2. **Does the company have a responsibility and/or liability?**

   Yes. Once Midge notified her supervisor the first time, the company should have acted. Its failure to do so could be a future liability problem because a member of management (her supervisor) was aware of the employee's problem, yet did nothing. The supervisor should have taken Midge's first notification seriously and contacted Personnel or some other authority inside the company.

3. **What should the supervisor do now?**

   The supervisor should notify Personnel or some authority about this matter. The appropriate authority in the company should begin an investigation and take appropriate action. It is likely that until the offending employee is removed, the supervisor may need to work out some alternative arrangement for completing the inventory checks. For example, the supervisor may accompany her to the Shipping Office. Or her visits could be scheduled at times when Susan is instructed to be away from the office. Or the inventory checking tasks could be assigned to another employee.

Case 9 ✍

They Came from Docu-Max

Background Information

All six individuals in the clerical and correspondence pool were overjoyed when the long-awaited announcement was finally made: Their department would be getting the new Docu-Max Automated Production system. This word processing system was the best in the field and would make everyone's job easier.

Beverly Marshall, a typist who had entered the department 18 months ago, had worked with a Docu-Max system at her former place of employment. She was particularly looking forward to the semiprivate workstations each typist would receive. An attractive 28-year-old mother who had returned to work after her youngest child began school, Beverly liked her work and got along well with her coworkers.

Installation of the system began on Monday of the week following the announcement and was expected to take a full week to finish. The Docu-Max Corporation assigned three of their installation technicians to do the job. The technicians were men in their mid-thirties. Once the basic plans are agreed to, these men work without any on-site supervision from Docu-Max.

The installation process required the technicians to assemble the workstations and supporting terminals, as well as to route and hook up the various electrical and cable systems that made the system work. Consequently, the technicians had to maneuver and climb around the office as people were trying to do their jobs. Just how disturbing this activity could be became apparent to Beverly on Monday, when two of the technicians spent a lot of time working around her desk. Initially, Beverly exchanged friendly conversation with them, but by the afternoon, their constant comments and interruptions were becoming annoying. Beverly was glad when the day was over.

On Tuesday, the situation became unbearable. At about 9:00 a.m., the two technicians walked in with coffee and stood near Beverly's desk. She smiled, said "Good morning," and tried to go back to work.

Speaking casually, without lowering his voice, one of the men began telling the other about the incredible time he had the night before with a woman he "picked up" in a bar. Beverly could hear every word as, for about ten minutes, he described his sexual encounter in explicit detail. The other man laughed along and offered a variety of suggestive comments. Beverly tried her best to pretend that she was paying no attention to them.

The men finally started working. They spent an hour stringing cables around Beverly's desk. A number of times one man or the other touched Beverly as they maneuvered the cables and the equipment around her desk.

Just before lunch, they began trading comments *about Beverly* within her hearing. "I'd sure like to try a repeat of last night with her," said one, laughing.

"Do you think she'd be good in bed?" asked the other.

47

"Are you kidding? She wouldn't have to be, 'cause I'd do all the work," replied the first.

One of the men moved his ladder next to Beverly's desk. He climbed to the top, looking down at Beverly the entire time. As he opened the ceiling tile, he said, "Hey doll, why don't you go out with me tonight and let me show you what sex is supposed to be about?"

Beverly quickly got up and went to the ladies room. There, she ran into June Boston, one of her coworkers. Beverly was very upset and told June what had been going on. They spent some time talking about the situation.

Shortly thereafter, on her way back from a meeting, Mary Bowers, Beverly's supervisor, passed June's desk. June was telling a coworker about Beverly's story. Mary heard the gist of it.

Walking back to her office, Mary reflected on the past two days. She had noticed that the installers were unusually busy around Beverly's desk, but she had not realized how serious things were. When Mary reached her office, she sat down at her desk and wondered what she should do.

CASE QUESTIONS

1. Is this a case of sexual harassment? Does the company or supervisor have any responsibility in this matter?

2. Mary Bowers knows she must act on the problem.

   a) What should she do in regard to Beverly?
   b) What should she do in regard to the installers?

3. Should Mary have acted more quickly? If so, in what way?

The Management Training Tool Kit: 35 Exercises to Prepare Managers for the Challenges They Face Every Day, ©2012 HRD Press.
Published by AMACOM Books, American Management Association, www.amanet.org.

Case Discussion:
They Came from Docu-Max

Summary

As a clerical worker in the correspondence pool, Beverly Marshall was pleased to hear that her employer had decided to introduce a Docu-Max Automated Production system. Beverly, an attractive mother returning to work after a recent birth, had used a Docu-Max system at her previous employer's company, and she knew how much easier it could make the job. However, her job became much more difficult when, on the first day of the installation process, the Docu-Max technicians assigned to install the system kept working about her desk, talking to her continually and interrupting her work. The next day, the two technicians intentionally stood near her desk while one told the other about his sexual exploits the night before. For the entire morning, both men worked near her, even touching her on occasion. Shortly before lunch, they began talking about her in explicit sexual terms. One man finally propositioned her. She ran off to the ladies' room, feeling very upset, and told a coworker what had been happening. Beverly's boss, Mary Bowers, later overheard the coworker relating the details of the incident to another employee in the department.

Answers to Case Questions

1. **Is this a case of sexual harassment? Does the company or supervisor have a responsibility in this matter?**

   Yes to both questions. Sexual harassment is unwanted sexual advances or requests for sexual favors or any conduct of a sexual nature that creates a hostile, intimidating, or offensive work environment. Such advances can come from others who are not employees of the organization if they are present under the direction of company management.

   Based on Beverly's reactions and statements, it is clear that she did not welcome the actions of the Docu-Max employees; she also finds those actions offensive.

   Now that Mary Bowers has constructive knowledge of this episode, she should take action.

2. **Mary Bowers knows she must act on the problem.**

   a) **What should she do in regard to Beverly?**

      Mary should meet with Beverly privately as soon as possible to listen to Beverly's story. She should seek verification of this information, if possible, from any coworkers.

      Another option would be to send Beverly back to her workstation while Mary stays close by in order to personally verify any further harassment.

      Either way, Beverly should be assigned to another work station until the matter is resolved.

b) What should she do in regard to the technicians?

If Mary can obtain proof of harassment, she should do the following:

- Order them from the work site immediately
- Notify the person in charge of the Docu-Max contract inside the company
- Contact Docu-Max supervisors
- Notify Personnel or the appropriate authority

3. Should Mary have acted more quickly? If so, in what way?

This is a judgment call. Mary noticed a high level of activity near Beverly's desk earlier. But this is not a clear indication of a problem. On the other hand, Mary was not present at any point during the installation.

Case 10 ✍

He's Just Not the Same

Background Information

In the same month, Bill Connors turned 47 years old and began the start of his 11th year with the Bay State Service Corporation. Bay State Service provided various maintenance, cleaning, and repair services for apartment complexes in the greater metropolitan area. Bill had been hired initially to work in the Transportation Department as a driver. About four years ago, he moved to a job in the mail room. Even though the mail room job required more lifting and carrying, in Bill's mind, the salary increase more than justified the added work.

It turned out to be a good move for him. The pay increase really helped, and although the pace was hectic, Bill kept up with the work. His performance was always acceptable; he consistently showed up on time and was always busy.

When on vacation last year, his tenth year with Bay State, Bill injured himself in a nasty fall while hiking during a family camping trip. His family took him directly to the hospital, where an X-ray showed both a broken leg and ankle. The doctor told him he could not return to work until the bones were fully mended, a five-week rest at the minimum. However, just before he was scheduled to go back to work, he called his boss, Ken Pierce, to tell him that since he was still in a lot of pain, the doctor wanted to put a brace on his leg and keep him home a little longer.

Bill returned to work three weeks later, but things were not the same, and they did not improve much in the following year. Bill's problems all went back to his injury. There was some indication that the leg and ankle breaks had not been set properly. Bill eventually had to wear a substantial leg brace, and he occasionally walked with a cane. It became obvious that he could not keep up his former pace of lifting and delivering the bulky boxes, bags, and packages that had to be delivered throughout the company. Ken tried to give him as much desk work as possible, but there remained a substantial backlog of items that just weren't being delivered on a timely basis.

Now, not long after the anniversary of Bill's 11th year with the company, some of his fellow employees in the mail room, particularly the newer ones, are beginning to complain to Ken about the extra work they have to do; they claim to be doing twice the work Bill does, at about half his salary.

Ken knows he will be doing Bill's performance appraisal in about three months. Based on the production problems in his department, he really wants to just "tell it like it is" and get rid of Bill. After all, Bill can no longer keep up, and it is a physical job. Ken wonders whether he could suggest that Bill be given a transfer. However, Ken is not optimistic that a transfer can be arranged.

The Management Training Tool Kit: 35 Exercises to Prepare Managers for the Challenges They Face Every Day, ©2012 HRD Press.
Published by AMACOM Books, American Management Association, www.amanet.org.

CASE QUESTIONS

1. What legal regulations apply to this situation?

2. Can Ken Pierce (Bill's supervisor) legally fire Bill?

3. Should the supervisor try to terminate Bill?

4. What kinds of options does Bill's supervisor have for dealing with this matter? What should Bill's supervisor do?

The Management Training Tool Kit: 35 Exercises to Prepare Managers for the Challenges They Face Every Day, ©2012 HRD Press.
Published by AMACOM Books, American Management Association, www.amanet.org.

Case Discussion:
He's Just Not the Same

Summary

Bill Connor, 47, has been with Bay State Service Corporation for 11 years. About four years ago, Bill was promoted from the Transportation Department to the mail room. The mail room job involved lifting and carrying boxes of supplies for distribution throughout the organization. For three years, Bill consistently did an acceptable job in this capacity.

Last year, during a vacation camping trip, Bill broke his leg and ankle in a nasty fall. The doctor who set his leg told him he needed five weeks of rest. However, just before returning to work, Bill called and notified his boss, Ken Pierce, that he had to stay out a little longer because the leg was not mending properly.

When he did return to work, Bill could not maintain his pre-injury pace of lifting and delivery. Eventually, he had to wear a leg brace and use a cane. His boss gave him as much desk work as possible, but a backlog of undelivered materials began to build up. Other employees in the mail room are now complaining that they are working harder and making less money than Bill.

Bill has a performance appraisal due in three months. His supervisor would like to just tell him the truth and terminate his employment. Short of that, he would like to suggest that Bill be given a transfer, although he is not optimistic that a transfer can be arranged.

Answers to Case Questions

1. What legal regulations apply to this situation?

The applicable laws affecting disabled employees do exempt smaller and nonfederal contractor employers. Although the exact size and nature of Bay State Service is not clear, this case assumes that Bay State is covered by these laws.

There are two main laws that could apply. The Rehabilitation Act of 1973 generally prohibits employment practices that discriminate on the basis of disability. The Americans with Disabilities Act of 1990 extends that basic protection by detailing certain procedures for adjusting employment to accommodate workers with disabilities. There may be state or local laws that apply also.

Under these laws, a person is considered disabled if (in part) that person has a physical impairment that substantially limits one or more major life activities. In this case, Bill would clearly be considered as having a disability. Consequently, he would be protected by these laws.

2. Can Ken Pierce (Bill's supervisor) legally fire Bill?

This is something of a trick question. Under the general provisions of the Employment-at-Will Doctrine, an employer has the right to hire and fire at will, so in that sense, Ken does have the right to fire Bill. However, in this case, Bill enjoys certain protections that, if violated, could be legally contested. Ken's preferable course of action would be to follow the legally defined guidelines, which could end up in Bill's termination.

3. Should the supervisor try to terminate Bill?

A first answer to this question is as much an ethical judgment as a legal one. Bill has been a consistent and presumably loyal employee for Bay State Service for more than a decade. He still wants to work and, with some assistance, appears able to do so. Does Bay State want to give up such a valuable employee so easily?

Beyond this consideration, Ken should first exhaust some other alternatives before moving to a termination (see Question 4).

4. What kinds of options does Bill's supervisor have for dealing with this matter? What should Bill's supervisor do?

Under the Americans with Disabilities Act, *qualified* individuals cannot be discriminated against and denied employment because of their disability. A qualified person is someone who has the skills for the job and who, with or without a *reasonable accommodation,* can perform the *essential functions* of the job.

In this situation, Ken should work closely with his Human Resources Department. The first steps in this case would be to determine what the "essential functions" of the job are. These functions define the basic nature and purpose of the position; they should focus on the outcomes of the job, not necessarily on how tasks are performed.

For example, in this case, is the essential function of the position to distribute bulk or is it to make sure information and materials are in sufficient supply in each department? The answer to this question should be recorded in a job description.

Second, can Ken make certain reasonable accommodations to the job that would allow Bill to perform the job? In part, Ken has already made certain adjustments by letting Bill do as much desk work as possible. Reasonable accommodations could include adjustments such as job restructuring, modifying a work schedule, and acquiring or modifying equipment or devices. Such accommodations are required unless they involve significant difficulty or expense to the employer (this is referred to as *undue hardship*). What is significant depends in part on the size and resources of the employer.

Here, because Bay State seems to be relatively large, an additional level of accommodation might be expected. For example, there are at least two accommodations that Bay State might be expected to take: (a) a permanent restructuring of the job to give Bill more of an administrative set of duties or to allow him to deliver only smaller items to local sites; (b) the purchasing of equipment that Bill can operate that will do the lifting and carrying. There might be other feasible alternatives.

While these steps seem excessive, their application can be done relatively directly and deliberately. They can certainly be completed within the three-month period before Bill's performance appraisal is due. If after these actions Bill is still unable to perform the job, and no other alternatives are possible, Bill can be terminated.

Case 11 ✍️

Special Checking Is Handed a Loss

Background Information

Sammy Benson supervised the Special Check Sorting Unit of the Greater Downtown Bank and Trust Company for over two years. The Special Check Sorting Unit processed all the "special" checks that came into the bank, such as odd-sized, foreign, or damaged checks. Once the checks were sent to his unit, they were manually interpreted, recorded, entered into the appropriate account transactions, and filed for return.

Sammy supervised three check sorting clerks in his department. These jobs were staffed by relatively untrained, entry-level individuals who had just graduated from high school. People who did well in this unit were often promoted into other positions in the bank. As such, turnover tended to be high, and there was a fairly steady stream of employees through this unit.

During the summer, Greater Downtown Bank hired low-income, disadvantaged young people for various jobs throughout the company as part of its Community Upbeat campaign. To participate in this effort, representatives from the Human Resources Department visited selected high schools to interview students. Since the students were already prescreened by the school, the interviews were little more than "get-acquainted" discussions. Last summer, Sammy's unit supplied one of the jobs in this effort.

Juanita Perez was hired in this context to work as a Special Check clerk. She was scheduled to begin working in June after graduating from the local vocational high school, where she maintained a C average. This was her first full-time job.

When Juanita reported to work in June, she was scared. It was not only her first day on the job, but the first time she had ever been in the bank. Nevertheless, she kept her courage and reported to the Human Resources Department as planned. After waiting in the lobby for a while, she was taken to a small meeting room where she and two other new hires were shown how to fill out and sign various forms and documents. Next, an administrative assistant read to the new hires a series of personnel policies about work schedules, breaks, overtime, pay secrecy, attendance, and benefits. She signed more forms, wondering what all this meant.

As the meeting drew to a close, Sammy Benson arrived after receiving a call from Human Resources. He and Juanita were introduced for the first time. Sammy escorted Juanita back to the Human Resources Department, showing her the bank's various offices and other departments. He gave her a quick tour of his area, introducing her to the other clerks as he went. Sammy was careful not to interrupt their work, however. He did not explain to Juanita what they were doing. It was obvious by the expressions on their faces that the employees were surprised to see her.

Sammy gave Juanita the job of processing foreign checks. He felt this task was the easiest job to learn and do correctly. During her first day on the job, Sammy spent about 15 minutes showing her the procedure: inspect, record, enter, adjust,

The Management Training Tool Kit: 35 Exercises to Prepare Managers for the Challenges They Face Every Day, ©2012 HRD Press.
Published by AMACOM Books, American Management Association, www.amanet.org.

file. Since he had to prepare for a meeting later that day, that was all the time he could spend with her.

By the end of the first week, Juanita seemed to be getting the hang of things: she came to work on time, stayed busy, and was fairly pleasant and easy to get along with. Sammy intended to spend as much time as possible with her during this period; however, because she seemed to catch on quickly and he was very busy, he saw her only occasionally over the next few weeks. He would ask how the work was going, if she was getting it done, and whether she needed any help. Juanita would always smile and say everything was going fine.

Then, after about a month, Juanita called in sick one day. A replacement was brought in, and as she looked through Juanita's desk for a notepad, she found what appeared to be a large pile of unfiled checks. When Sammy looked through the pile, he found that there were, in fact, quite a few unprocessed checks, some of which dated from Juanita's first day on the job. As they were the more unusual kinds of checks the department handled, Sammy assumed that she apparently had not known how to process them. Unfortunately, the combined value of these checks totaled around $65,000. The bank had lost the "float" value on them, and Sammy knew that customer complaints would be coming in soon.

Sammy expected Juanita to come back to work the following day, and he wondered if he should write up a warning notice for her immediately.

CASE QUESTIONS

1. What is the work maturity or competence level of Juanita Perez? What kind of supervisory behaviors should Sammy have used with her?

2. Describe the adequacy of the orientation process that Juanita received. What kind of orientation procedure should Sammy have used with her?

3. How should Sammy respond to the problem of the unprocessed special checks?

4. Sammy is considering issuing a formal written warning notice to Juanita upon her return. Is this an appropriate action to take?

The Management Training Tool Kit: 35 Exercises to Prepare Managers for the Challenges They Face Every Day, ©2012 HRD Press.
Published by AMACOM Books, American Management Association, www.amanet.org.

Case Discussion:
Special Checking Is Handed a Loss

Summary

Sammy Benson supervised Greater Downtown Bank's Special Check Sorting Unit, which processed odd-sized, foreign, and damaged checks. His staff of three were semiskilled recent high-school graduates. Sammy took on Juanita Perez one summer as part of the bank's Community Upbeat program. Juanita was hired and reported to the bank for a brief induction program. Sammy then arrived, met Juanita for the first time, and escorted her back to the department. After a quick tour and passing introductions, Sammy gave Juanita some basic instructions in her job. Juanita seemed to pick up on the work and fit in. After working there a month, Juanita called in sick one day. Her replacement discovered a large number of checks that Juanita had not processed. Sammy examined the checks and realized that Juanita had created substantial problems for the bank and its customers.

Answers to Case Questions

1. **What is the work maturity or competence level of Juanita Perez? What kind of supervisory behaviors should Sammy have used with her?**

   Juanita has a low level of work maturity: she has no prior work experience, no prior training in the task to which she is assigned, and limited ability to manage her work process. She does show an apparent commitment to working on time and well with others.

   Sammy should have used a directive leadership style with her. This would involve significant efforts to define work expectations, to train her in the task, and to check up on her performance regularly.

   Unfortunately, Sammy did not use the proper style of leadership with her. He did not establish standards for production nor for resolving problems. Although one would expect experienced and secure employees to bring problems to the attention of their boss, Juanita did not, perhaps thinking that she could correct them as she learned more. Ultimately, then, Sammy is responsible for Juanita's performance problem.

2. **Describe the adequacy of the orientation process that Juanita received. What kind of orientation procedure should Sammy have used with her?**

   There is a difference between an induction and orientation process. Induction involves the minimum steps of enrolling the new employee as a member of the organization. Orientation involves learning much more: the nature of the business, the function and operation of the department, working with the boss and other coworkers, personnel policies and procedures, and the like.

   In this sense, Juanita went through an induction process but received the bare minimum of an orientation process. The supervisor has the final responsibility for making sure new employees are properly oriented. Sammy did not meet this responsibility.

An effective orientation for Juanita would include instruction in what the banking business entailed and how this department's work fit into that business. It would also cover how to recognize checks of different types, what the function of this work involved, who the other people in the unit were, and so on. This process should have extended over several days and could have been delegated to a more senior member of the team who would serve as mentor to Juanita.

3. **How should Sammy respond to the problem of the unprocessed special checks?**

He should take care of any particularly critical special checks immediately. When Juanita returns, he should meet with her and let her know how the checks were discovered and ask for her explanation. It is desirable to make this discussion as nonpunitive as possible. Sammy could do this by conceding at the outset that he did not train Juanita adequately. Sammy should then undertake a better orientation process, along the lines noted above. He should also spend more time training Juanita by first going through the leftover checks to determine why she had problems with them.

4. **Sammy is considering issuing a formal written warning notice to Juanita upon her return. Is this an appropriate action to take?**

Given the circumstances, such action does not seem warranted.

Case 12 ✍

Beverly Comes Full Circle

Background Information

Beverly Wyman took her job as supervisor very seriously. Though only 33 years old and somewhat new to the company, she liked her work and believed she did a good job. Beverly was in charge of the Consumer Credit Sales Group of the First Union National Bank. She was in charge of seven credit sales representatives (CSRs). Her sales group was formed six months ago to aggressively sell and market the bank's various car, boat, and other personal loans. Beverly was promoted and became group supervisor shortly after the group was started, moving up from an assistant manager's job in the nearby Credit Analysis Section. Some problems in the Analysis Section kept her there longer than was anticipated, and she joined her sales group after it had already started operating.

Even though she was generally pleased with the progress her sales group was making, she did have a problem: Bob Watson. As she thought back, she knew why this was so painful now.

Back to the Beginning: Bob Watson

Three years ago, when Beverly joined First Union's Credit Analysis Section, Bob Watson was the chief credit analyst and her boss. He was then 41 and had been a First Union employee for 18 years. In this position, Bob was responsible for training all new junior analysts. Bob had long been a top credit analyst: he earned almost twice the net income as the next most productive employee in Credit Analysis. It was his exceptionally high level of productivity that allowed the division manager to look the other way whenever Bob had one of his occasional fits of moodiness. Indeed, although Bob was widely respected for his consumer credit talents, he was just as widely avoided for his unpredictable temperament and erratic work habits.

Beverly learned a lot about credit from Bob, and they got along well together—at least until Beverly started to equal Bob's record in Credit Analysis. That was about 18 months ago. It was around this same time that Bob seemed to undergo a change. There was a subtle but distinctive difference in how he worked: he maintained an adequate analytic volume, but he seemed drained of energy. Some employees thought the change was due to divorce.

Whatever the cause, Bob's idiosyncrasies now became a real problem and the change in his work became increasingly less subtle. He was absent from his desk frequently and for long periods. He would put in a couple of good hours of work a day and then spend the rest of the time listlessly wandering around. An exasperated department manager, Tony Ianelli, finally had to act, giving Bob a written disciplinary notice. Bob's wandering seemed to subside, but his underlying attitude—apathy, indifference, hostility—became even stronger.

59

Beverly Becomes Supervisor

All these problems with Bob occurred before Beverly was made supervisor. Tony explained the situation to Beverly before he hired her, because Bob had now been transferred a second time to the newly formed Consumer Credit Sales group as senior representative. He was given the temporary duty of running the sales group until the permanent supervisor—soon revealed as being Beverly—arrived. Bob's job was the same kind of position he had filled in Credit Analysis: to train the sales reps in Beverly's sales group. But now, he was working for Beverly instead of Beverly for him.

During the job interview, Tony told Beverly, "We considered Bob for the credit sales manager's job, but decided we just didn't think he would work out as a supervisor at this time. We did think that more responsibility might be what he needs, though, so we made him senior representative."

Tony told Beverly that as senior representative, Bob would have the three newest sales reps work directly for him as trainees. Thus, Beverly would supervise Bob and the other three CSRs directly; she would supervise the three trainee reps indirectly through Bob. The chart below shows the organization of First Union's Consumer Credit Sales Division.

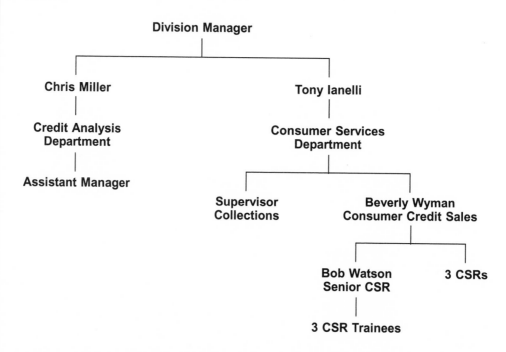

Four months after Beverly moved into the supervisory position, she was facing a number of problems with Bob Watson. She believed that Bob could consistently be a top performer if only he could get over his "attitude problem." She thought that although Bob realized he blew his chance for a management job because of his erratic performance, he still felt cheated. He applied for other jobs in the bank at

The Management Training Tool Kit: 35 Exercises to Prepare Managers for the Challenges They Face Every Day, ©2012 HRD Press.
Published by AMACOM Books, American Management Association, www.amanet.org.

every opportunity. He still did an average job, although his sales performance had been falling for the past few months. Beverly was also concerned about his work method: he seemed to do the easiest sales jobs first and then give up too quickly on the more demanding and challenging opportunities. So while he still performed fairly well, his work was just not up to his potential.

Beverly was experiencing other difficulties with Bob, too. She was alarmed at the way his attitude was affecting the three trainees who worked under him. She sensed their resentment of her. A recent incident was still troubling her. She had asked Bob to explain to the trainees a new procedure that all the CSRs had to follow. Beverly felt it was a good system and hoped that Bob would introduce it well. However, she was distressed to hear one of the trainees complain about the "crappy, stupid new procedure" they had to complete. Beverly could only imagine how Bob must have explained it.

Another of Beverly's concerns was Bob's almost total indifference to her. She could remember a number of times that Bob had gone over her head to talk with Tony directly about some questions or concerns. The rest of the time, he seemed to ignore the plans she and Tony made. When asked for his input, he usually complained that the idea would never work.

In particular, he seemed totally resistant to changing some of his practices and bringing them into accord with the newly revised Consumer Credit Protection Laws. Potentially this was Beverly's biggest problem because mistakes under this new law could cost the bank a lot of money in lawsuits and penalties. She had circulated a flier announcing the changes to all employees, but it appeared that Bob had not even read it. With his experience and ability, Bob was able to work in the gray area between superselling and regulatory violation fairly easily. He did not, however, seem to appreciate the danger in which he was putting the bank, and his trainees were picking up his questionable tactics.

Altogether, Bob was consuming an enormous amount of Beverly's time and energy. Her productivity was being hampered by Bob's continual problems. Even worse, Tony Ianelli seemed unwilling to take any drastic action, and Beverly felt her ability to act was limited by Tony's sensitivity to "front-office" pressure to keep Bob around. Even though she had not yet broached the subject with Tony, firing Bob did not seem possible.

As her fourth month as a supervisor drew to a close, Beverly sat at her desk, looking at one of Bob's recent sales reports. She shook her head slowly, noticing more of the same errors. Beverly knew that although the problem was not an emergency, it needed correcting. Beverly wondered to herself, "What can I do?"

The Management Training Tool Kit: 35 Exercises to Prepare Managers for the Challenges They Face Every Day, ©2012 HRD Press.
Published by AMACOM Books, American Management Association, www.amanet.org.

CASE QUESTIONS

1. Describe the problem(s) that Beverly faces as a supervisor. Identify what specific performance improvement results she should seek.

2. What key rule(s) or principle(s) should Beverly use in solving the problem(s)?

3. Develop at least three different strategies or approaches for resolving this issue.

The Management Training Tool Kit: 35 Exercises to Prepare Managers for the Challenges They Face Every Day, ©2012 HRD Press.
Published by AMACOM Books, American Management Association, www.amanet.org.

Case Discussion:
Beverly Comes Full Circle

Summary

Four months ago, Beverly Wyman, 33, was promoted to the supervisor's job of a newly formed sales group. There were seven people in the sales group reporting to her, including Bob Watson (her boss when she first joined the company). Bob was about 10 years older than Beverly. He had been the highest performer in the company for a number of years, until Beverly began to equal his production about 18 months ago. Bob had a long history of personal moodiness and erratic behavior, though. When Beverly began to equal his performance, Bob's behavior became more problematic. He had finally been given a written disciplinary notice. Consequently, some of the behaviors changed, although the underlying "attitude" problems of apathy, indifference, and hostility did not.

When Beverly was promoted to head up the sales group, Bob Watson was given the job of supervising three trainees in the department in addition to sales production tasks. Now, four months later, Bob had developed into a major supervisory problem for her. Beverly currently had several concerns about Bob's work:

- He gave up on tougher sales chores.
- He was infecting his trainees with a negative attitude about her and the operations of her department.
- He ignored her authority and plans and was not a constructive contributor to the department.
- He circumvented new regulations and laws, putting the company at risk.

In short, Bob was consuming quite a bit of Beverly's time and attention, while performing far below his potential. He was continually seeking to find another position in the company. It seemed that the "front office" would be protective of him; Beverly assumed that they would not allow him to be fired.

Answers to Case Questions

1. **Describe the problem(s) that Beverly faces as a supervisor. Identify what specific performance improvement results she should seek.**

   Beverly's problem is how to respond to a rather unique problem employee: he is a long-term employee who is very knowledgeable and capable. But, his work behaviors are just not acceptable—and may actually be risky to the business. He seems to be unreceptive to Beverly's supervision of him.

   It is generally unproductive to speculate on what Bob's "motivation" or "psychological" problems are. It is difficult to accurately identify those underlying motivations when there is limited evidence of what is behind them, and in some ways, using such a "theory" merely "explains" what he is doing without helping Beverly deal with it.

   Instead, it is preferable to identify what kinds of improvements in his behaviors Beverly wishes to see. These improvements correspond to the problems noted above; they are listed below in likely order of importance to Beverly:

63

- Complying with the new laws and regulations
- Accepting her authority and becoming a constructive contributor
- Being a positive and constructive force with the trainees
- Displaying more perseverance in working on tougher sales

2. What key rule(s) or principle(s) should Beverly use in solving the problem(s)?

Beverly should keep in mind several rules or principles when approaching these problems:

1. In the final analysis, it is Bob's responsibility to comply with the standards of performance set. While Beverly may be experiencing the effects of the problem, it is Bob's problem. Both he and Beverly need to understand that it is his decision about what will happen.

2. Beverly needs to be clear about what those standards are and what will happen if he does not meet those standards.

3. She should not make assumptions about what can or cannot be done with Bob. She should prepare the way for action by initiating discussions with the "front office" to obtain its agreement to support her actions. This includes reaching an agreement with her boss, Tony Ianelli, regarding stopping his end-run behaviors.

4. Open and direct communication with Bob is necessary. In that regard, offering support and assistance is appropriate.

3. Develop at least three different strategies or approaches for resolving this issue.

There are a number of strategies Beverly could pursue. They are not mutually exclusive.

1. Reach an agreement with the "front office" about how Bob will be treated. This will involve notifying "the office" of the potential liabilities the company faces and the productivity problems that are likely. She should also present a plan for dealing with Bob, which could include a transfer if firing is not possible.

2. Meet with Bob to set expectations and note future consequences. Beverly should make it clear to Bob what her standards of performance are. She needs to point out that the responsibility for all future outcomes are his; that is, he needs to understand that it is now his problem. She needs to state what will happen to him if he does not meet those standards. This conversation should be noted and kept as a record in her files. It would be very appropriate to have Tony Ianelli sit in on this meeting.

3. Beverly could refer Bob to the firm's Employee Assistance Program if one were available.

4. An alternative approach to a meeting with Bob would be more of a counseling session. In this case, Beverly could use assertive communication and active listening skills to raise the problems at hand for discussion purposes. In such a meeting, she could begin by using "I" messages to raise problems she's experiencing and then ask for his reaction. By actively listening to him, the underlying reasons for his behavior may become discussable. Plans could be made to address his concerns. It may be that she could work with him to make a transfer to another area.

Other options may also exist.

Case 13 🖎

It Was Really So Simple

Background Information

Brenda Galway leaned back in her chair, sighed heavily, and slowly rubbed her eyes in big circular motions. "I don't need all this aggravation," she thought to herself. She had just finished reviewing the report she had requested from her new employee, Bill Stanley. The entire report was incorrect and would have to be redone.

Brenda supervised Unit B of the Audit Department. The Unit B team had earned the nickname of the "Mod Squad" because the team was given unusual, special audit assignments that cropped up. Unit B also had ongoing audit duties over certain operations departments within the company. The five auditing specialists in Unit B had to complete certain reports every month on those operational units. Normally, this workload was manageable enough. Unfortunately, this was not one of those times.

About three weeks ago, Brenda's manager, John Rockland, gave her a major project to complete in three weeks. The "rush priority" nature of the project stemmed from the decision of the company's Executive Management Committee to implement a new type of auditing procedure and install a program. In large part, this meant adapting to an automated information system. Currently, most of the information the company needed and used was being collected and processed manually. In effect, the new system required the auditors to switch from being high-priced clerks to being information system managers. The auditors would be able to examine, "test," and display information more quickly, easily, and clearly—so, at least, was the thinking of Executive Management when it authorized the new procedures. Brenda's assignment was to complete an implementation plan for this new system in three weeks.

At the meeting during which he gave her the assignment, John told Brenda: "Look Brenda, I know it's short notice and that you've got those operations reports due out soon, but you need to get your staff working on this project now. You know I'll do whatever I can to help."

John had paused a minute, leaning against the doorway. "Why not let that new guy, what's his name. . . Bill Stanley? Let Bill Stanley start working on it."

Brenda could see no alternative. "I guess you're right," she said. "I'll get him on it today."

John had been referring to the new employee Brenda had hired just last month. Bill Stanley graduated two years ago with a degree in accounting and had worked as a junior auditor at a competitor since then. During the interview process, Brenda told him that he would have to be a self-starter and that she expected him to pick up on the work fairly quickly.

She now thought back to her words during the interview: "Look, we're very busy here, and we get the plum assignments. I can't babysit you. I'll show you your desk and introduce you to the team members. You're going to have to take care of yourself. Of course, I'm here to help and my door's always open. But you'll have to

65

The Management Training Tool Kit: 35 Exercises to Prepare Managers for the Challenges They Face Every Day, ©2012 HRD Press.
Published by AMACOM Books, American Management Association, www.amanet.org.

pin me down and get me when you need my help. After that, you're on your own." Brenda had prided herself on her direct, no-nonsense, up-front communication style.

Bill Stanley seemed to agree with her philosophy. He replied, "Sure, that's great. I like to work on my own anyways."

In fact, Bill Stanley had not been Brenda's first choice for the open position in her department. She was looking for someone who had both auditing and computer experience in addition to a strong background in accounting. Unfortunately, she was unable to pay the salary that the few applicants with that background wanted. Bill Stanley was the best remaining choice, even though he had very limited auditing and computer experience.

Bill had accepted the job and had been doing as well as could be expected. During his first week on the job, he was placed on an existing audit project and had managed to perform effectively according to the project leader. He seemed to get along well with the other "Mod Squad" team members and was fairly eager to work on the project, although Brenda seldom saw him stay after quitting time.

Brenda had called Bill into her office shortly after receiving the new assignment from her boss. She told him about the project and gave him the deadline. She repeated that her door was always open if he needed help. Bill seemed honored that she had selected him. He tried to ask her for some details about the kinds of plans he needed to work out. Brenda repeated that it was a simple project plan. After Bill's third question along these lines, Brenda said, with a little irritation in her voice, "Look, you can figure this out. Unless you have any other big questions, I've got to get ready for a meeting."

Bill answered that he had no other questions.

Brenda had drawn the meeting to a close with the remark, "Keep in touch."

In the two weeks that followed, Brenda continued to be as busy as usual. She occasionally saw Bill in the office. While passing through, she would sometimes stop, put her head through the door, and ask how things were coming. Bill would always say, "Fine."

On two occasions, Bill asked to see her. In the first meeting, about two days after receiving the assignment, he tried to get her to explain what exactly she was looking for in the report. He produced a detailed outline. Brenda looked it over and made a broad, vague response. Her irritation at having to tell him exactly what to do showed after about 15 minutes. In the second meeting, he asked for some general guidance and help on many of the specifics of the project. She wondered, at one point, why he didn't look up the answers to some of these questions himself. She had to cut their meeting short in order to attend another meeting. After the second meeting, she had no further contact with Bill.

It was now three weeks since she gave Bill the assignment. The deadline had arrived, and Bill had submitted the report on time, dropping it off on her desk at 5 o'clock, on his way home. Looking it over, she had easily seen that it was incorrect. Oh, it was all there, alright; it was just wrong.

For a long time she continued to rub her eyes, as if doing so would change the contents of the report and it would be correct when she looked at it again.

The Management Training Tool Kit: 35 Exercises to Prepare Managers for the Challenges They Face Every Day, ©2012 HRD Press.
Published by AMACOM Books, American Management Association, www.amanet.org.

Brenda thought to herself, "Why didn't he come in and check it out with me to make sure that he was doing it right, especially after he completed this first part? It was really so simple and I took so long to explain it."

CASE QUESTIONS

1. What is the problem?

2. What should Brenda do about the faulty report?

3. How should she have supervised Bill on this project?

The Management Training Tool Kit: 35 Exercises to Prepare Managers for the Challenges They Face Every Day, ©2012 HRD Press.
Published by AMACOM Books, American Management Association, www.amanet.org.

The Management Training Tool Kit

Case Discussion:
It Was Really So Simple

Summary

As a supervisor of the high-profile "Mod Squad" Unit in the Auditing Department, Brenda Galway prided herself on her no-nonsense, direct, and independent management style. She wanted hard-charging, competent auditing personnel who could operate independently.

Her most recent hire, Bill Stanley, had seemed to accept these conditions when she interviewed him for the job. He had acquired some background in this field, but was not the most qualified applicant Brenda had spoken with. Nevertheless, because Brenda was unable to pay the salary that fully qualified applicants wanted, Bill ended up with the job.

Brenda was not pleased when she learned that the Executive Management Committee of the company had authorized a conversion of the auditing process from a manual to a computerized system. She was given the responsibility of preparing a project implementation plan within three weeks. Brenda and her experienced staff were consumed with ongoing audits that could not be dropped, and she was forced to give the new project to Bill Stanley.

When giving Bill the assignment, Brenda made it clear that he was on his own but could call on her at any time. Subsequently on two occasions, Bill asked for more details about what she wanted in the report, but he did not receive much in the way of specific information from Brenda. Quite often she saw him in passing, and he always indicated that things were fine. Otherwise, Brenda had no involvement with him on the project. Bill turned the project in on time, but it was incorrect and needed to be redone.

Answers to Case Questions

1. What is the problem?

There are really two problems here: the apparent problem and the underlying problem. The apparent problem is really a symptom of the underlying one and is the faulty report. The underlying problem is Brenda's inappropriate supervision of Bill on this project. She should attend to both problems.

The faulty report was ultimately a result of Brenda's failure to provide adequate direction, support, and control to Bill—that is a result of her poor supervision of Bill on the task.

2. What should Brenda do about the faulty report?

Since the ultimate reason for the faulty report is Brenda's, she should not penalize or denigrate Bill because of the problem. Rather she should take responsibility for the problem. Depending on the degree of urgency involved and the extensiveness of the problems, she may need to make the corrections herself. However, if at all possible, she should use this situation as a coaching opportunity with Bill. This means spending time explaining to him what the report should include.

In a meeting with Bill, she should admit that she did not give him the direction he needed and emphasize that she is not being critical of his work. Instead, she should detail what the report should contain and where it needs to be corrected. She should work with him to make the adjustments.

Even if she cannot work with him because of deadlines, she should have the same meeting with him as soon as possible.

3. How should she have supervised Bill on this project?

Bill had a moderate amount of competence for completing this task. His above-average motivation to work independently was offset by limited experience with computers and very limited experience putting together a work plan.

Therefore, Brenda should have used a combined directive and participative approach. When giving Bill the assignment, she should have clearly and specifically detailed what the structure of the plan should look like. She should have provided examples, demonstrations, and any published support materials.

Next, she should have set up follow-through meetings with Bill to review progress. At first, these meetings should have been scheduled daily or every other day. She should have looked over Bill's progress on the project at those points, given him tips and direction, and answered any questions. As he developed more confidence, the meetings could be spaced out more infrequently, although never more than three to five days apart.

Case 14 ✍

Pain in Claims

Background Information

Sandy Jones supervises a clerical and secretarial pool of eight employees at the American Standard Insurance Company. Her group is responsible for typing and filing the insurance claims and registrations for Standard's customers in the Southern region. It is high-volume work that, although requiring speed and accuracy, is often tedious.

Sandy is proud of her unit because the members get the work done well. Generally, Sandy enjoys her job and likes the people she works with. Most of her subordinates are young women who recently graduated from high school, some from the same school. By and large, this is their first regular job.

Sandy has one headache, though, and that headache is Katherine Bruskowicz. Katherine is a very good worker, perhaps quicker and more accurate than anyone else in the unit. She learned the job very quickly and now finishes her work before the others. The only problem with Katherine, as Sandy told a friend at lunch one day, is that "she's just a pain in the ass."

"For example," Sandy said, "Katherine talks all the time. Now I know the work can be tedious, and I let the staff talk as long as they get their work done, but Katherine can get really loud at times, especially when I'm gone. I know, I've gotten complaints from others." Sandy is worried that Katherine's talkativeness may become an annoyance and distraction to the other employees.

Even more disturbing than the volume of her talk is the content. Katherine seems to delight in verbally harassing and intimidating the other employees in the unit. She brags about all the boyfriends she has. She will often mock how other employees dress or talk and will argue with them about doing certain tasks. She even picks on Sharon regularly, teasing her about her weight and lack of boyfriends.

Some of the employees in the unit have become accustomed to Katherine and can now take her in stride, although there are others who have a more difficult time dealing with her and whom she still upsets. In either case, the employees in the unit have to make adjustments, and morale in the unit stays low. Sandy is certain that if Katherine weren't there, everyone would be much happier.

Sandy has informally talked with Katherine a few times about these matters, and Katherine will behave for a day or two—then pick up again where she left off.

CASE QUESTIONS

1. Is there a problem? If so, what is it?

2. How should Sandy respond?

71

Case Discussion:
Pain in Claims

Summary

Sandy Jones supervises a group of eight clerks who do high-volume, relatively routine typing and filing tasks. The employees tend to be young women who recently graduated from high school. For most, this is their first job.

Katherine Bruskowicz is perhaps Sandy's best performer. However, she tends to be disruptive in the workplace. For example, she is a loud and incessant talker. She is also verbally abusive. She boasts about her boyfriends and belittles Sandy, who has no boyfriends. She also teases Sandy about being overweight.

Although some of the employees take her in stride, others are upset by her. Sandy believes that Katherine causes some morale problems. Sandy has "informally" talked with Katherine about these matters on several occasions. Katherine will make a temporary improvement, then revert to form.

Answers to Case Questions

1. Is there a problem? If so, what is it?

This is a borderline call. While Katherine is annoying, it is not clear that there are significant productivity problems as a result. Some of her coworkers have adjusted to her. Furthermore, Katherine's job performance is evidently good.

On the other hand, Katherine's talking and rudeness do seem to heighten the level of tension and reduce the group's morale.

Considering the above, the question is whether Katherine's verbal behavior is an annoyance or a problem. This is a determination that each supervisor needs to make individually.

However, Sandy should watch for signs of hostility or stress directed at Katherine. She should also pay attention to the turnover of her staff. If either increases, Sandy will need to act so that the work problems caused by Katherine will not grow even more serious and the work environment further deteriorate.

2. How should Sandy respond?

It is not clear that Sandy should do much more than she is already doing. Certainly, as noted above, she should begin monitoring the mood of her group more closely. She should also continue to correct Katherine when she gets out of hand.

Sandy should also schedule a formal meeting with Katherine to discuss the problem of her loud and abusive behaviors.

Unless matters become worse, it is not clear that Katherine's behavior is of sufficient nature to justify a formal disciplinary procedure.

Case 15 ✍

Don't Let Her Get Behind You
Part 1—*Making Adjustments—NOT!*

Background Information

Lynecia Jackson was a supervisor of the Secretarial Support Unit in Monumental Services Corporation. The primary responsibility of her unit was to provide secretarial support to the three groups making up the Administrative Support Division: the Property Services, Purchasing, and Auditing departments (see the organizational chart below).

Administrative Support Division

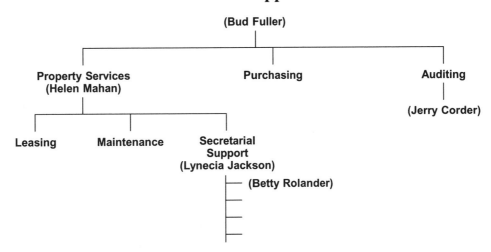

Lynecia supervised the four secretaries in the unit. During her first year as supervisor, she faced a major personnel problem with Betty Rolander. Betty, 28, had been with Monumental for almost six years, holding various clerical and secretarial positions during her career there.

Betty had a "bad attitude" problem that drove Lynecia crazy: Betty was haughty, abrasive, and even antagonistic when dealing with other people. For example, when Lynecia noted problems or errors with her work, Betty would fly off the handle and become very defensive.

Lynecia told her friend Bob Erhard about Betty one day: "At first, I thought it was just me, you know, that Betty just didn't like me. But I checked her personnel file. Almost every one of her previous bosses had written complaints about the poor way she dealt with people, but they never did anything about it—and now she's my problem."

The roots of Lynecia's problem with Betty went back to the reorganization that had led to Lynecia's promotion. Shortly before Lynecia was made supervisor, about a year ago, the centralized secretarial support system in use at Monumental's Headquarters office was disbanded and replaced by a more traditional structure. Under

73

the prior, centralized system, all the secretaries in Headquarters were hired, managed, and controlled through a single manager, Helen Mahan, even though the secretaries worked in other departments. Betty Rolander had worked directly for Helen Mahan. They liked each other and got along well together, and Betty became a lawyer and devoted follower of Helen's.

However, recurring problems with this centralized system caused its demise. Under the reorganized system, secretaries were reassigned to each department and reported to the manager of each division. Helen Mahan was reassigned as manager of a newly formed Property Services Department. To take the sting out of this reorganization, Helen retained the management duties of the secretarial staff in the Administrative Services Division. Lynecia Jackson was made supervisor of the secretaries and reported to Helen Mahan.

In reviewing some of the items in Betty's personnel file, Lynecia learned that Betty had applied for the supervisory job, but had been turned down. When Lynecia saw this, she thought it explained Betty's hostile behavior. She also hoped that the hostility would subside as they began to work more closely together. Unfortunately, she was wrong. After a few months on the job, the problems with Betty grew worse, not better.

One of the most significant incidents that confirmed this trend developed when Lynecia received a complaint from Neal Coleman. Neal was an executive vice president in charge of Monumental's Operations Division. One day, he called Lynecia directly to complain about the rude way Betty had talked to Miriam, his secretary, during a phone call that morning. As he explained it to Lynecia, "She insulted and argued with her. Miriam became very upset, and I don't blame her. You better do something about her." He was angry.

Lynecia thanked him for the message, and then called Betty into her office. Lynecia told her: "We have a problem, Betty. I've just received a complaint from Neal Coleman about how you spoke to his secretary this morning."

"What did you say in reply?" Betty shot back.

"I said I would take care of it. You just can't talk to people like that," Lynecia said.

"You did what?" Betty shouted back. "I can't believe it! I didn't do anything! This is your problem. You've got a bad attitude."

Lynecia was surprised at the intensity of Betty's reply but continued to explain what Neal had said and why Betty had to improve her phone manner. Betty continued to deny it forcefully. They argued like this for another five minutes. Throughout the entire discussion, Lynecia felt like she was the one on the carpet for making a mistake, not Betty. The discussion finally ended, but not cleanly or decisively.

CASE QUESTION

1. How should Lynecia have responded to the complaint from Neal Coleman?

74

The Management Training Tool Kit: 35 Exercises to Prepare Managers for the Challenges They Face Every Day, ©2012 HRD Press.
Published by AMACOM Books, American Management Association, www.amanet.org.

Part 2—*Lynecia's Ears Were Burning*

After this confrontation, Lynecia felt that Betty was *more* belligerent and hostile to her. Furthermore, as Lynecia found out later, Betty started talking about Lynecia behind her back. For example, Betty would complain to others, especially any managers who came by, about Lynecia's clothes, that she was away from her desk too much. or how her ability as a supervisor was poor. In staff meetings, Betty would try to sound as if she were speaking for everyone else by making comments such as, "We're really having these problems with you," or "None of us thinks that's a good idea." These remarks were then followed by a discussion of all that Lynecia was supposedly doing wrong. Lynecia finally stopped having staff meetings because of Betty's tirades and criticism.

Betty also complained about Lynecia to Helen Mahan (her old boss and Lynecia's current boss). Soon thereafter, Helen gave Lynecia some "friendly advice": Lynecia should stay closer to her desk. Shaken and unsure, Lynecia accepted the advice and limited her work to her desk area.

CASE QUESTIONS

1. Is Betty guilty of insubordination?

2. Given what Lynecia knows at this point, what should she do?

The Management Training Tool Kit: 35 Exercises to Prepare Managers for the Challenges They Face Every Day, ©2012 HRD Press.
Published by AMACOM Books, American Management Association, www.amanet.org.

Part 3—*The Ice Breaks*

Part of Lynecia's job was to support and serve Jerry Corder's Auditing Department, which, in turn, depended on her help a great deal. However, Lynecia told Jerry one day that she could not help him anymore because of complaints that she was away from her desk too much. Jerry couldn't believe what he had heard, and marched into Bud Fuller's office with Lynecia in tow. Bud listened to Jerry's complaint and then asked Lynecia to explain. She told him about Helen's "advice" and Betty's complaint. It was a Thursday afternoon.

The following Monday morning, Bud Fuller called a meeting of his management staff in the Administrative Services Division and made the following announcements:

1. Lynecia Jackson and her staff no longer report to Helen Mahan, but directly to Bud Fuller.

2. Lynecia is the supervisor in charge of that unit, and she is not away from her desk too much.

3. If there are problems with Lynecia, they should be brought first to Lynecia's attention, and if that is not satisfactory, then to Bud.

Both Helen and Betty were shocked by the announcements. Betty seemed to improve for a week or two, but eventually began criticizing Lynecia again. During this time, Lynecia told Betty to train the floater secretary who was going to sit in for Betty during her upcoming vacation. Betty indicated she could finish the training quickly, but by the end of that week, Betty had not yet trained the floater. Indeed, Betty simply ignored her.

Learning this, Lynecia canceled Betty's vacation leave on the grounds that she did not prepare her replacement as directed. Lynecia gave Betty a chance to regain her vacation, though. If Betty could train her replacement in the week before her scheduled vacation, she could have it back. Betty finally did this—and did it fairly well. During that week, though, Lynecia received permission from Bud Fuller to give Betty a written disciplinary notice.

ASSIGNMENT

Given this information, you are to conduct a disciplinary meeting with Betty.
Prepare a written disciplinary notice and use it during your discussion.

The Management Training Tool Kit: 35 Exercises to Prepare Managers for the Challenges They Face Every Day, ©2012 HRD Press.
Published by AMACOM Books, American Management Association, www.amanet.org.

Case Discussion:
Don't Let Her Get Behind You

Summary: Part 1—Making Adjustments—NOT!

For about a year, Lynecia Jackson had supervised four secretaries who served the three departments within the Administrative Support Division of the Monumental Services Corporation. During that time, she had run into a major problem in the form of Betty Rolander, 28, who had been with Monumental for almost six years in various secretarial positions.

Lynecia was bothered by Betty's arrogant and abrasive manner of dealing with other people. When looking through her personnel file, Lynecia discovered that Betty's previous managers had had similar concerns, although no one had taken strong action.

Lynecia traced her problem back to the company reorganization that had taken place about a year ago. At that time, the centralized secretarial support system in the Headquarters building had been replaced by a decentralized system. The previous system had been managed by Helen Mahan. Betty worked for Helen and became a loyal fan of hers. When the company reorganized, Helen was made a department manager, becoming Lynecia's boss, and Betty then began working for Lynecia. Subsequently, the working relationship between Lynecia and Betty had gone downhill.

One day, Lynecia received a call from Neal Coleman, an executive vice president, who complained about the insulting way Betty had spoken to his secretary on the phone that morning. Lynecia called Betty into her office and admonished her for speaking rudely to Neal's secretary. The discussion was argumentative and unproductive.

Answers to Case Question

1. **How should Lynecia have responded to the complaint from Neal Coleman?**

   Lynecia should have apologized to Neal Coleman and indicated that she would look into the problem immediately. She should have called Miriam to apologize and hear directly from her what happened. She next should have asked Betty to describe how she remembered the conversation. Assuming that the complaint against Betty was well founded, Lynecia should have given her feedback on what exactly she did that created problems.

   She also should have restated the standards of appropriate phone courtesy. It would be acceptable to have Betty call Neal Coleman's secretary to apologize, thus reinforcing the importance of courtesy. Lynecia may or may not want to be present during that conversation. Lynecia should also make a note or memo of this conversation and keep it in a working file.

Summary: Part 2—Lynecia's Ears Were Burning

After the Neal Coleman incident, Betty became more belligerent to Lynecia. For example, she dominated Lynecia's staff meetings and criticized Lynecia's job performance, wording her comments so that it sounded as if she was speaking for everyone present. She would talk about Lynecia behind her back, especially to managers who came through the area. (Lynecia found this out later.) Finally, Betty complained to Helen Mahan, who was Lynecia's boss. Helen suggested that Lynecia spend more time at her desk. Lynecia was shaken by this and did so. As a result, she began to limit her work to her desk area.

Answers to Case Question

1. **Is Betty guilty of insubordination?**

   There are two issues here: first, what is *insubordination,* and second, is she guilty?

   First, *insubordination* is usually understood to mean an unwillingness to submit to a legitimate authority. It appears that Betty has not refused to do tasks she has been instructed to do. Instead, she is contemptuous and spreads dissention. This is a gray area: while she may technically not be insubordinate, her actions in spirit seem insubordinate.

   Second, Lynecia has no direct evidence of Betty talking behind her back. She only knows this from hearsay. But Lynecia does see Betty disrupt meetings and try to convince others that Lynecia is ineffective. Again, there is a gray area here. She is clearly acting in a disruptive fashion, even if her actions may technically not be insubordinate.

2. **Given what Lynecia knows at this point, what should she do?**

   Lynecia may have a difficult time making a charge of insubordination stick. Nonetheless, Lynecia is faced with an employee apparently intent on creating grief. Lynecia should meet with Betty to establish certain standards of conduct, such as bringing any problems she has to Lynecia's attention first. This new standard could lay the standard for insubordination charges in the future if Betty persists in complaining about Lynecia without first mentioning the problems to Lynecia.

   Lynecia should reinstitute staff meetings. She needs to exercise more control over the meetings, especially when Betty begins speaking for everyone else. She can do this, for example, by polling the other people present after Betty makes such a claim. She can set the agenda for the meetings ahead of time to control what is discussed. She can give Betty assignments to fix "problems" she brings up. She can encourage other employees to disagree with whatever Betty wants to argue about. Finally, she can censure Betty for disrupting her meetings if all else fails.

   Lynecia needs Helen Mahan to clarify what Lynecia's duties are and what authority Lynecia has to act in pursuit of those duties. Lynecia should also raise the issue of Betty's "end-run" communications to Helen. Lynecia should seek clarification from Helen about the proper kinds of communication "channels" that should run among Helen, Lynecia, and Betty.

Summary: Part 3—The Ice Breaks

Lynecia told Jerry Corder, head of the Auditing Department, which she served, that Helen Mahan effectively restricted what Lynecia could do, and as a result, she could not serve Jerry in the manner to which he had been accustomed. Jerry exploded and talked to the division manager, Bud Fuller. By the start of the following week, Bud had removed Lynecia's unit from Helen's supervision. He now had Lynecia report directly to him and gave her full supervisory authority. Consequently, Betty's performance improved slightly.

In anticipation of Betty's forthcoming vacation, Lynecia directed Betty to train a replacement floater secretary. Essentially, Betty ignored that directive. As a result, Lynecia canceled Betty's vacation but gave her the opportunity to earn a reprieve if she could still train the replacement in time. Betty did so. At the same time, Lynecia received permission to issue a formal disciplinary notice to Betty.

Assignment

Given this information, you are to conduct a disciplinary meeting with Betty. Prepare a written disciplinary notice and use it during your discussion.

In general, it is clear now that Betty has been insubordinate in refusing to train her temporary replacement. Given the history of this employee's performance in the department, the discussion with Betty should make it clear that her job with Monumental will be on the line if there are any further examples of disruptive or insubordinate behavior on her part.

Case 16 ✍

Kathy's Temper

Background Information

Gene Jenkins has been acting supervisor of the Accounts Servicing Department of Wilson's for the past two months. Wilson's is one of the premier department store chains in the region, and the Accounts Servicing Department is responsible for maintaining, updating, and adjusting the credit accounts of Wilson's 20,000 charge customers. Gene was moved into this position after the previous supervisor left abruptly in anticipation of a reorganization. Gene was told to keep the operation running until final decisions about a reorganization could be made.

There are four account service representatives in the department. All four are women in their mid to late 20s. They have been in the department for an average of five years. Each representative is responsible for approximately 5,000 accounts. In order to complete their duties, they must often deal with other employees throughout the chain of stores, as well as with the customers themselves. Thus, in addition to the skills needed to manage, adjust, and service the accounts, the "reps" must be very polite and tactful when talking with others.

Before being promoted into his current supervisory capacity, Gene worked as a rep for three years. During that time, he mastered the job and knew that with a little concentration and discipline, it could be both challenging and satisfying. Therefore, he could not quite understand Kathy Showers.

Kathy, 27 and single, has been in the department for a little more than two years. During that time, she learned the job well. She can process the paperwork quickly and without error and, indeed, will often finish her work before anyone else. Because Kathy commutes to work over a long distance via public transit, she often arrives early. This explains in part why she finishes her work ahead of time: she frequently starts working a half-hour early.

In spite of a good record, though, Kathy's performance has started to slip recently. In fact, Kathy has become a big problem for Gene since he became acting supervisor. As one of her coworkers put it when complaining about Kathy the other day: "She's enough to drive you crazy."

Kathy has become very unpredictable and moody. When a customer or coworker irritates her, her first reaction is to give everyone the silent treatment. Since her behavior is so obvious and affects everyone who works in the same office space with her, the tension level in the office has risen significantly. When dealing with customers or other employees over the phone, she tends to be abrupt and curt to the point of being rude. Or, when she must deal in person with someone, she will often sigh impatiently as the person approaches her desk or simply continue talking on the phone while they wait. Gene has started receiving complaints from both customers and coworkers about this. And when she becomes really upset, she loses all control, shouting and sometimes swearing to whoever is nearby.

81

The problem seems to stem from Kathy's boyfriend. Gene learns from some of his coworkers that she makes personal phone calls to him several times during the day. On a number of different occasions, she has ended the phone conversation by yelling into, then slamming down, the phone. She then will jump up from her desk and leave for a long time, and when she returns, she will cry very easily when asked where she has been.

Some of the other employees in the department now "walk on tiptoes" around her, while a few others enjoy fighting with her. Although things are far from smooth and harmonious in the unit, Gene knows that something must be done but is not sure how to proceed.

CASE QUESTIONS

1. Is there a problem?

2. What should Gene do?

82

Case Discussion:
Kathy's Temper

Summary

As supervisor of the Accounts Servicing Unit, Gene Jenkins, manages four account service representatives. The reps must deal with both customers and employees frequently in a very tactful manner.

One rep, Kathy Showers, is very adept at her work. However, she appears to be going through a particularly difficult period with her boyfriend. As a result, she is often curt and abrupt, at times acting outright rude to others. Sometimes, she blows up in anger, shouting and swearing at whomever is nearby. She also talks to her boyfriend quite a bit on the phone. These conversations often end with her crying.

The tension in the office has increased dramatically, as coworkers try to tiptoe around her. Gene has been receiving some complaints.

Answers to Case Questions

1. Is there a problem?

Yes. Kathy's behavior in itself is not as productive as it can be. Furthermore, she is reducing the effectiveness of coworkers and detracting from the quality of the work of the department.

2. What should Gene do?

In this case, an otherwise competent employee has fallen to an unacceptable performance level because of a personal problem. Gene needs to get Kathy's behavior back to standard level while trying to help her deal with this situation.

Gene should meet with Kathy. He should note that Kathy's behaviors are creating some problems in specific ways and should restate the minimum standards of performance. He should also indicate his awareness of the difficulties she is having with her boyfriend and express a willingness to talk about the problem with her. If Kathy responds favorably, they could look into ways to help her through this period, including referral to employee assistance or perhaps temporary assignments to noncontact tasks.

Gene does need to make it clear, though, that Kathy is expected to meet the minimum standards.

Note to trainers: This situation can be used as the basis for a role play on employee counseling techniques.

Case 17 ✍

Forgetting Claims

Background Information

Betty Warren, 36, has been supervisor of the Claims Adjustment Unit for the State Department of Unemployment Insurance for over two and a half years. The Claims Adjustment Unit is responsible for processing claimant appeals concerning either incorrect payments or administrative judgments made on their application. Although the work was often frustrating and difficult, Betty nonetheless enjoyed her job and her work until June Williams joined the unit. That is why the current situation with June is so irritating to Betty.

When the department went through a cost-cutting reorganization not long ago, Betty inherited June Williams, a 54-year-old employee who had been with the agency for over 28 years. June was pleasant enough to work with and could do certain parts of her job fairly well, but, as Betty came to discover, she just could not seem to master one of the key tasks of the unit that all employees needed to know: how to complete the Adjustment Determination Form 1293.

The ADF 1293 is the basic form used to record the information and decisions made on each applicant's appeal. The procedure associated with this form includes the following steps:

1. Verify that all the information supplied on lines 6–10 and 14–27 are correct.

2. Look up the individual's eligibility criteria from the appropriate table in the state code book.

3. Compute the personal exemption rate by using the standard formula: (number of dependents * 1200) + weeks unemployed rate, where weeks unemployed rate = number of weeks unemployed * 0.25.

4. Compare the results of steps 2 and 3, and record on the attached Decision Report Sheet.

5. Make a decision and enter reasoning in section 5 of the form.

On the average, Claims Adjustment clerks are expected to complete 15 of these forms a day. Betty had found from her experience that it typically took about four to six weeks for new employees to reach this level of performance.

On June's first day with the unit, Betty showed her the procedure for completing the form. June watched as Betty completed each step. She took no notes, only smiled and nodded her head as Betty worked through the procedure. At the conclusion of the training, she asked no questions and said that she understood. Already a little late for a meeting, Betty left June at her desk to start work.

Three days later, Betty received a bundle of ADF 1293 forms that June had processed, but they were all incorrect. She called June into her office and explained the procedure again. June watched very closely, nodding and smiling and looking

85

very intently at what Betty was doing. Again, June asked no questions. Betty finished the demonstration, and June returned to her desk.

Over the next two weeks, Betty continued to receive incorrect forms that June had processed. Now, after three weeks on the job, June is barely doing 10 forms a day correctly. However, she has been making some slight progress and the number of incorrect forms has been falling.

Betty thinks, "Boy, June sure has a bad memory. She simply can't recall what she was told. She's been bluffing about learning what I told her."

CASE QUESTIONS

1. What standards should Betty set for June during her first month on the job?

2. Did Betty do a good job training June? Is June stupid?

3. How should Betty have trained June? Create a training plan for June.

4. Make a performance aide for the ADF 1293 procedure (you can make up any details that you need to as long as they are consistent with the procedure outlined in the case).

The Management Training Tool Kit: 35 Exercises to Prepare Managers for the Challenges They Face Every Day, ©2012 HRD Press.
Published by AMACOM Books, American Management Association, www.amanet.org.

Case Discussion:
Forgetting Claims

Summary

Betty Warren supervises the Claims Adjustment Unit for the State Department of Unemployment Insurance. One central task performed by her unit is the processing of Adjustment Determination Form (ADF) 1293s. The steps for processing this form include the following:

1. Verifying information supplied in certain blocks
2. Checking the applicant's eligibility criteria
3. Computing the personal exemption rate
4. Comparing steps 2 and 3, and recording the answer on an attached sheet
5. Making a decision and recording the rationale for it

The Claims Adjustment clerks are expected to complete 15 of these forms a day.

Not long ago, Betty inherited June Williams, 54, as a result of a cost-cutting reorganization. June had been with the department for more than 28 years and was easy to work with. After some instruction in the ADF 1293 tasks, June started processing the forms.

Three days later, Betty had a bundle of ADF 1293 forms returned to her. They were all done by June and were all incorrect. Betty instructed June again in the procedure. But, not unexpectedly, June's work continued to be returned because of errors. Now, after three weeks in the unit, June is only processing a few forms correctly each day.

Answers to Case Questions

1. **What standards should Betty set for June during her first month on the job?**

   Betty should set a standard of performance that is approximately at the level to which new employees are expected to perform. This number may be based on her past experience or determined after she consults with other employees. In all likelihood, the number set would be lower than the standard of performance expected of a proficient employee.

   What Betty should be trying to do is fit the standards of performance to a typical learning curve for that task. The learning curve would describe how long it takes an employee to reach a set standard of performance.

2. **Did Betty do a good job training June? Is June being dense?**

   Betty did not do a good job training June. She just demonstrated the basic procedure with her on June's first day. She did not insist that June take notes nor did she provide June with on-the-job instruction or any performance aides to refer to. She evidently did not follow through with June after the first day.

   The question of June's intelligence is not a helpful one at this point. Almost anyone in a new situation will feel stress, which will in turn lower their learning effectiveness. June probably does not want to appear dumb or slow; unfortunately, by acting in this way and not asking questions, she is creating exactly the impression she wants to avoid.

87

3. **How should Betty have trained June? Create a training plan for June.**

The first part of the training process for June should have included an orientation to the unit and the personnel. Betty should have explained the work that was being done and the larger work plan of the unit. She should have gone through a demonstration of the process as she did; however, Betty should have done several other things too:

- Required June to take notes
- Required June to complete the ADF 1293s on her own while she watched
- Assigned another employee to be June's coach during the learning process
- Provided a set of instructional exercises for completing the ADF 1293
- Provided a performance aide for June to use
- Communicated the standards of performance during this training period, including a projection of when June should begin to become fully proficient
- Check in with June regularly to see how she was progressing

4. **Make a performance aide for the ADF 1293 procedure (you can make up any details that you need to as long as they are consistent with the procedure outlined in the case).**

A simplified version of an ADF 1293, shown on the next page, is available online. A performance aide is a visual guide and worksheet for how to complete the form. Participants might create any number of displays. A key point, though, is that any display should be tested and verified prior to use.

ADJUSTMENT DETERMINATION FORM 1293 ✍

Section 1

Date: _____

1. Name: _____

2. Address: _____

3. City: _____ 4. State: _____ 5. ZIP: _____

Section 2

6. Current earned income: $ _____

7. Other sources of income: $ _____

8. Savings in bank: $ _____

9. Assistance received: $ _____

10. *Total* $ _____

11. Eligibility status code: _____

12. Prior determination: _____

13. Reason: _____

Section 3

14. Last employer: _____

15. Address: _____

16. Phone: ( ) _____

17. Date hired: _____ 18. Date released: _____

19. Reason for separation: _____

20. Time unemployed: _____

21. Personal exemption (number of dependents): _____

22. Personal exemption rate: *   1,200.00

Section 4

23. Number of weeks unemployed: _____

24. Factor: *   0.25

25. Weeks unemployed rate: _____

26. Weeks unemployed rate (from 25):   +   .00

27. Recalculated eligibility criteria: _____

Section 5

28. Review determination decision: ❑ Accept   ❑ Decline

29. Reason: _____

89

The Management Training Tool Kit: 35 Exercises to Prepare Managers for the Challenges They Face Every Day, ©2012 HRD Press.
Published by AMACOM Books, American Management Association, www.amanet.org.

Case 18 ✍

Answering the Phone

Background Information

Jim Mullens likes supervising the Customer Service Unit. This unit is responsible for updating customer accounts and files, as well as for providing information to customers and other employees. Typically, the customer service representatives (CSRs) whom he supervises answer questions about the services offered, provide information about the customer's account, and modify the files so that they are up to date and correct. This unit was formed only recently to handle the increasing volume of direct customer calls more efficiently by using the newly installed online customer information system.

Unfortunately, planning for the new unit was not done well. The online computer system was purchased and installed before the actual operations people were brought in. As a result, Jim was given the responsibility for getting the unit up and running within one week. He had to make some quick personnel selections and take care of a lot of administrative details within a short period of time.

Now, three weeks after receiving the assignment, Jim feels quite a sense of accomplishment. He has been lucky that things have worked out as well as they have. In fact, the only thing Jim is concerned with now is the way in which his reps handle customers over the phone.

Jim knows that good telephone etiquette is essential to the successful accomplishment of his unit's mission, yet his reps use many different styles in answering the phone and do not follow basic rules. For example, the reps commonly neglect to put customers on hold while they search for information; when asking questions, they do not explain the reason for the inquiry; they do not verify information; and, at times, they may react defensively when they don't know the answers. These are the major—but not the only—things they do wrong.

Jim knows that he must train them in the techniques of proper phone etiquette. There is no available training program to which he can send his personnel. Therefore, he must provide the training and coaching to the reps while they are on the job.

ASSIGNMENT

Prepare a training plan for Jim to use.

The Management Training Tool Kit: 35 Exercises to Prepare Managers for the Challenges They Face Every Day, ©2012 HRD Press.
Published by AMACOM Books, American Management Association, www.amanet.org.

Case Discussion:
Answering the Phone

Summary

Jim Mullens is given the task of staffing the new Customer Service Unit. This unit was created in response to a newly installed online customer information system. Now the customer service representatives (CSRs) in the unit are expected to handle customer phone calls and answer any of the full range of questions the customers might have.

Unfortunately, Jim was not including in planning for the unit, and he only had one week to complete his assignment. He was fortunate to have recruited enough people to get the operation going, but after three weeks, he is now concerned about how the reps are answering the phones. He has noticed that the reps make a variety of mistakes in phone etiquette, such as not putting the caller on hold when necessary, not explaining what they are doing, not verifying information, and acting defensively.

He knows they need training but realizes that he must do it himself while the reps are on the job.

Assignment

Prepare a training plan for Jim to use.

There are two fundamental steps Jim should follow in preparing a training plan: defining desired standards of CSR performance and creating learning experiences to train the CSRs to meet those standards. Hence, a training plan should contain information on those two broad domains. A more detailed plan could include a job analysis, creation of learning objectives, a needs assessment, a training curriculum, and a means of evaluation. This exercise could be used as a basis for the latter, more detailed plan. However, in a more applied sense, completing the two general steps would be sufficient for Jim's purposes. The particular details of each step are addressed below.

Performance Standards. A reasonable set of performance standards for the CSR job would likely include the following.

The CSR should

- efficiently access all customer information using the customer information system;
- accurately interpret the customer information system to report customer information;
- enter information into the system correctly;
- follow established phone procedures and etiquette; and
- deal constructively with any conflict or dispute.

These standards are listed in an approximate order of learning acquisition for a training plan. That is, before acceptable phone performance can be expected, CSRs must first be able to use the customer information system.

Note: A more detailed training planning approach could include a more formal job analysis. Jim might hold a meeting with the CSRs to define their exact job duties. Further, at this meeting or at a subsequent one, he could complete a needs assessment by identifying what this group needs to learn. Because Jim should expect some turnover in his group, a complete training plan like the one under development here should be prepared for use now and in the future.

Training Plan. Jim's training plan must take into account certain parameters: the training will be done at the worksite; the training may occur during regular service hours; the training will need to use the existing system; and, due to practical constraints, the training will probably not be conducted with everyone together at the same time. Considering these parameters, it is important to work out the plan so that the training program can be grafted onto the existing production process.

There would be two major subsets of the training: how to use the customer information system and how to use the phone in communicating with customers.

A. Using the system

Jim could create a series of exercises by using the existing customer files. He could also create a set of "dummy" customer files (clearly identified as such). Either way, he could set up a series of inquiries, interpretations, and input exercises to work the trainees through a progressively more complicated set of assignments.

This training could be presented in the form of self-instructional exercises. For example, Jim could prepare a booklet of pages with different assignments. For a brief period of time each day and on a rotating schedule, the trainees could be put "off line" to complete certain exercises. A training schedule reflecting this plan would be easy to create.

Jim should make sure to verify the accurate completion of each segment by reviewing the assignments and directly observing the trainees. He could even give each trainee a "final" exam—that is, a set of new assignments that they must complete while he watches.

B. Using the phone

Once mastery of the system is achieved, the CSRs should be trained in using a standard phone protocol. This should begin by communicating what the phone standards are. The etiquette problems Jim has observed would be addressed simply by preparing a list of standards and presenting it to the CSRs. He should regularly monitor phone behaviors to make sure the standards are being met.

The training process should include handling difficult customer calls. Jim should identify the most common issues that create conflicts. He should then prepare training vignettes around these issues. He should also identify the procedure that should be used to respond to these calls. A likely procedure might include active listening, restating customer requests, offering alternatives, fixing problems quickly, and verifying solutions.

The training could proceed as follows: Jim would prepare the procedure as a training handout. In a general meeting, Jim could review and demonstrate these skills. Either in that meeting or in individualized sessions, either Jim or another CSR would be the "customer" and go through role-play exercises, which would be based on the vignettes, with the CSR. He could then coach each CSR on how they used the skills in responding to the situation.

Case 19 ✍

Good News, Bad News
Part 1—*The $15.00 Mistake*

Background Information

Ted Banacek smiled as the "I've got some good news, and I've got some bad news" refrain kept repeating itself in his mind. "I can really appreciate it now," he thought to himself as he sat at his desk, looking out the window at the empty parking lot.

The good news was that Ted had recently been promoted to the assistant manager's job at State Bank's Westbury Mall Branch. The Westbury Mall Branch, one of the larger, busier branches in State Bank's network, had seven full-time tellers and three full-time new accounts personnel. It was something of an honor to be made assistant manager after starting at the bank less than a year ago.

For the past four months, Ted had really enjoyed his duties: he was learning about new aspects of banking, meeting customers, and working with employees. Ted was particularly pleased that his time in the bank's Management Trainee Program had finally paid off. Once in an assistant manager's spot, a branch manager's job was just a matter of time. He wanted to do this job exceptionally well.

The bad news was that the job was a lot tougher than he had imagined, and now he was sitting in boiling water with his job on the line—or so he thought. He was upset, nervous, and just plain confused. As he stared out the window, he recalled how it all began.

From the first day he worked for her, Ted thought his manager, Janice Schuster, was a good boss: she was easy to talk to and gave Ted attention and advice. Over time, she had given him increasing responsibility for running the day-to-day operations of the branch as she made more and more sales calls on customers outside the branch. They both grew extremely confident of Ted's ability, so there was no concern or fanfare when Janice began her vacation two weeks ago. During her first week away, things went smoothly, and Ted had experienced no major problems.

He thought the second week would be like the first, and it had been, very briefly, until about 10:30 on Monday morning. A customer had just found a charge on his checking account. The charge was four months old—well beyond the normal grace period established by the bank. The customer explained, "I just got around to looking at my statements and found this charge. I've been a good customer here for a long time and don't think I should have to pay for this one item. I'd like the amount refunded to me."

Ted had handled these situations before. He knew the fee was a legitimate one and that the notification period had elapsed. He also knew that the bank wanted to increase fee income. He felt strongly that there

95

was no mistake on the bank's part and declined to reverse the charge. Ted used his best business manner to explain the situation to the customer nicely, but the customer was not pleased. Obviously upset, the customer finally left Ted's desk and went to the teller line to cash a check.

Ted shrugged his shoulders. "If you'd have brought this in sooner," he said to himself, "we might have done something. Tough luck." He then busied himself with other things.

About 10 minutes later, Ted scanned the lobby during a work break. He noticed that the displeased customer was talking to one of the tellers and Judy Miller, a new accounts clerk. He could see that it was an animated discussion. At one point, the customer pointed in Ted's direction. Both the teller and Judy shook their heads in agreement. He noticed that other customers and tellers seemed to be listening in on their conversation. He shrugged his shoulders and got back to work.

Later that day, after the branch closed, one of the tellers asked to talk to Ted privately. Ted listened as she told him, "I think you should know what Judy was talking about with that customer today. The customer was complaining that you did not refund her $15.00 charge. Judy just happened to overhear the complaint and then started agreeing with the customer that you should have refunded the money and that it was dumb that you didn't. I was embarrassed because some of the other customers heard it, too. Some of the tellers also heard the tale, and now they're making jokes and complaining about your '$15.00 mistake'!"

Ted said, "Thanks for telling me." He felt his stomach knot a little.

CASE QUESTIONS

1. Is there a problem here worth dealing with? If yes, what is the problem and how should it be handled? If no, why not?

2. What kinds of customer service standards should exist for all employees in situations like this? How should those standards be communicated and enforced?

3. Is Judy Miller "guilty" of insubordination?

4. Should Ted respond to the situation? If yes, how?

The Management Training Tool Kit: 35 Exercises to Prepare Managers for the Challenges They Face Every Day, ©2012 HRD Press.
Published by AMACOM Books, American Management Association, www.amanet.org.

Case Discussion:
Good News, Bad News: Part 1—The $15.00 Mistake

Summary: Part 1—The $15.00 Mistake

As a recent graduate of State Bank's Management Trainee Program, Ted Banacek had been promoted to the assistant manager's job at one of the busier branch offices. One week when Ted's manager was away on vacation, a customer asked for a refund on a charge for $15.00 made to her checking account. After reviewing the details, Ted decided not to make the refund for various legitimate reasons. The customer, unhappy with the decision, went to the teller line to finish some other business.

Shortly thereafter, Ted noticed that the customer was talking with Judy Miller, a new accounts clerk. It appeared that they were talking about Ted and that other employees were listening in. Ted did not think any more about it.

Later that day, after the branch was closed, a teller came into Ted's office and told him that Judy had been openly critical of the way Ted had handled the customer. Now, after hearing Judy's remarks, other employees were making fun of Ted's "$15.00 mistake."

Answers to Case Questions

1. **Is there a problem here worth dealing with? If yes, what is the problem and how should it be handled? If no, why not?**

   There are several potential problems here that call for action either immediately or in the future.

   The first issue is whether Ted should have refunded the $15.00 fee. This is in large part a matter of company business policy. In this case, the fees were part of the agreement and the customer's notification was beyond the grace period. Whether the bank has a policy on customer satisfaction to supersede fee collection is the key issue here.

   The second problem reveals itself in Judy Miller's apparent ignorance of the bank's fee collection business goals. It appears that the staff is not aware of those goals either or, if they are, they do not accept them. This is a potential problem that needs to be corrected soon.

   The most obvious problem, though, is the behavior Judy Miller exhibited when she openly spoke ill of another employee rather than seeking to fix the problem. She also stirred ridicule of the manager among the rest of the employees. This situation should be dealt with directly and immediately.

2. **What kinds of customer service standards should exist for all employees in situations like this? How should those standards be communicated and enforced?**

   There are two main standards that apply here. The first has to do with how customer fee complaints should be handled. This should be a matter of bank policy and basically involves the decision about whether fee collection is more important than customer satisfaction. Whatever the decision, front-line service employees should be notified of it and trained in how to apply this policy.

97

The second standard has to do with how employees should react to customer problems "caused" by another employee. There are two kinds of behavior that should be included in this standard. First, employees should respect one another, and one employee should not "bad-mouth" another employee in front of a customer, much less other employees. Second, the employee hearing the complaint should either work at resolving the problem or support and explain the decision if it is not possible to fix it. Again, all employees should be notified of this standard and trained in how to apply it. Violations of this important action should be grounds for disciplinary action, depending on its severity and magnitude.

3. Is Judy Miller "guilty" of insubordination?

At this point, it appears that Judy has violated what should be common standards of customer contact. However, there are two issues: does Judy know what those standards are, and did she in fact do what was alleged? These actions are serious. However, "insubordination" usually means an employee's willful and open refusal to comply with legitimate directives issued by a superior. Technically, that does not seem to be what happened. Judy was not being insubordinate in this case.

4. Should Ted respond to this situation? If yes, how?

Since Judy's actions are potentially very serious, Ted should investigate this situation more closely. It would be appropriate to informally ask another teller what happened. If there was a general confirmation of what Judy did, Ted should meet with Judy. During that meeting, he should indicate that he has learned from several sources about what she has done and that he would like to hear her explanation. He should state the standards of behavior expected and that he does not appreciate what she did. He should indicate that in future situations, he expects her to either support his decision or to bring it to his attention by offering a solution.

Ted should then call a meeting with the staff to review the bank's policy on collecting fees and to review this particular incident. He can, with good humor, refer to the "mistake" and indicate that it was not a mistake but rather an application of the bank's policy. He could also use the meeting as a time to conduct some training in how to handle similar situations.

Note to trainers: This situation would be a good role-playing opportunity for trainees.

Case 20 ✍

Good News, Bad News
Part 2—*Judy, Judy, Judy*

Background Information

Four months ago, Ted Banacek completed State Bank's Management Trainee Program and was assigned as assistant manager of the busy Westbury Mall Branch. Pleased with Ted and confident of his abilities, his manager took a two-week vacation. The first week went smoothly for Ted, but on Monday of the second week a problem developed when a customer asked Ted to refund a $15.00 fee that was four months old. Complying with bank policy, Ted refused politely. The customer, angry over the refusal, later engaged several branch employees, including a new accounts clerk, Judy Miller, in a conversation in which Judy belittled Ted and inspired ridicule of Ted among the tellers in the bank.

Even though, at age 27, Judy Miller was just a few years older than Ted Banacek, she had been working at State Bank almost five times as long. While Ted was completing his college degree, Judy married, had two children, and started working at State Bank as a teller. Smart and hardworking, she had slowly but surely progressed up the ranks. She had been a new accounts clerk for a full year before Ted even came to the Westbury Mall Branch.

Judy went through a divorce not long ago. Needing more income and wanting a more professional career, she was very interested in being promoted and thought she was as capable as the next person for a manager's job. She also let it be known to everyone in the branch that she thought that she—and not Ted—should have been given the assistant manager's job.

Whenever Ted dealt with Judy, he could detect a resistant, competitive edge to her. However, he never felt that their working relationship was impaired. He could recall many examples when they worked closely together to solve a customer problem or complete a special project.

Indeed, until the recent incident with the customer regarding the matter of the $15.00 refund, Ted had no reason to give Judy Miller a second thought. If Ted had any insecurity, it stemmed from his lack of teller experience: in the bank's Management Trainee Program, the trainees did not work as tellers. He believed that anyone, including Judy, who had experience as a teller had a real advantage, and he was very self-conscious about this area of weakness.

Late Monday afternoon, as he looked out at the bank's empty parking lot, Ted wondered whether he should do something to respond to what had happened with Judy and the customer. He decided to let things ride, not rock the boat, and see if the problem might simply go away.

On Tuesday morning, he came to work with a "clean slate." Fortunately, it looked like it would be a quiet, slow day. He diligently got to work. In going through his mail, he spotted a document that Judy had sent to Operations—and that had been completed incorrectly.

99

There were only a few customers in the lobby. He went to Judy's desk; she was chatting with a coworker as they processed some paperwork.

Ted began: "Judy, I just opened this document back from downtown. It's the one you filled out yesterday. Unfortunately, you did it incorrectly." He carefully continued, "It's okay that you made a mistake. It's a long and complicated procedure. Let me show you how to do it correctly."

Ted proceeded to show Judy how to fill out the document, thinking he was helping her. He also considered this his way of saying, "I'm not letting yesterday's events with the customer bother us. Let's continue to work together." Yet, as he talked to her, Ted could sense that Judy was uncomfortable and defensive.

Finally, Judy blurted out an explanation of why the mistake occurred: "I was rushed, there were a lot of customers." The other back-office person piped in that there had been a big rush of people yesterday.

Ted finished the discussion by asking Judy to redo the form and send it back to Operations. However, for the remainder of the day, Ted sensed that Judy—along with some of the other employees—was angry at him and avoiding him. By the end of the day, Ted knew that something was wrong with the staff, and his spirits started to sink.

Now it is Wednesday, which picks up where Tuesday ended. By mid-morning, though, the situation has gotten worse. "Something is definitely wrong here," Ted tells himself. "There's too much whispering among the tellers and no one is talking with me." The tension in the branch office is almost tangible. He starts to think that he is failing: "I'm blowing this. If I don't do something, I'll lose my job."

He calls one of his friends, Sandy McGill, a manager at another branch, and explains what has happened. "What should I do, Sandy? I feel like things are out of control. Should I say anything, call a branch meeting, talk to Judy individually, or what? I need some help."

Sandy can tell that Ted is anxious and very concerned.

CASE QUESTIONS

1. What kind of problem does Ted have here?

2. What event(s) occurred that led to this state of affairs?

3. How should Ted proceed? What should he do now?

The Management Training Tool Kit: 35 Exercises to Prepare Managers for the Challenges They Face Every Day, ©2012 HRD Press.
Published by AMACOM Books, American Management Association, www.amanet.org.

Case Discussion:
Good News, Bad News: Part 2—Judy, Judy, Judy

Summary: Part 2—Judy, Judy, Judy

Although only slightly older than Ted, Judy had been a bank employee much longer. She started as a teller and by virtue of hard work, progressed up the career ladder. Because of a recent divorce, Judy wanted more money and a more professional position. When Ted was given the assistant manager's job, she let everyone know that she felt she should have been given the job, not Ted. Nonetheless, Ted believed that they should be able to work together effectively enough. He felt a little insecure, though, because Judy had much more practical experience in day-to-day banking than he did.

Ted decided not to react to the "$15.00 mistake" incident. The next day, he discovered that a document that Judy had sent downtown had been returned because of an error. Ted brought the document to Judy's desk, where she was talking with a coworker. Ted interrupted, carefully pointed out Judy's error, and explained how she should have completed the document. For the rest of the day, Ted sensed that Judy, as well as several other employees, were avoiding him.

Now on the following day, the tension among the staff has grown even worse. Ted calls a friend who manages another branch and asks for help.

Answers to Case Questions

1. What kind of problem does Ted have here?

Ted has two problems. First, it appears that he has alienated Judy. Second, it also appears that at least some of the staff members are now supporting Judy and that there is a serious morale problem among some of the staff.

2. What event(s) occurred that led to this state of affairs?

The immediate cause was Ted's "friendly" coaching of Judy. Even though Ted did not see it as a humiliation, Judy experienced his coaching as a rebuke because it was played out in front of another employee. Ted violated a primary rule: correcting or coaching should generally be done in private.

This embarrassment undoubtedly fueled Judy's long simmering resentment of Ted. She apparently has been stirring up some other employees and turning them against Ted.

3. How should Ted proceed? What should he do now?

The focus of Ted's actions should be Judy. While he cannot expect to change her resentment of his promotion, he can expect her to behave in certain ways.

He should meet with Judy privately. It would be appropriate to begin the meeting by admitting that he was not as considerate as he should have been in dealing with the documentation problem. Second, he should note that he is concerned about the apparent morale problems Judy is creating among the staff. He should indicate that he does not know why Judy has a chip on her shoulder about him and that, although he is willing to talk about those reasons, he also expects her to behave properly. This means that if she has a problem with him, she should bring it to his attention and not spread dissension among the other employees. He should also indicate that if there is any further indication of her doing so, he will proceed with disciplinary action.

Note to trainers: This situation would be a good role-playing exercise.

Case 21 ✍

Good News, Bad News:
Part 3—*The Storm Breaks*

Background Information

As a recent graduate of State Bank's Management Trainee Program, Ted Banacek is now working as assistant manager in one of the busier branches. While his manager was away on vacation, a customer asked for a $15.00 service charge refund, which Ted politely refused. Shortly thereafter, the customer complained to Judy Miller, a new accounts clerk working for Ted. Judy, who believes that she should have been promoted into the position Ted now occupies, agreed with the customer and ridiculed Ted's decision. Ted ignored this incident, but the next day, he counseled Judy in front of another employee about a processing error she had made. Since then, it seems all the employees in the branch are giving Ted a cold shoulder. Ted feels he is failing as a manager and calls Sandy McGill, a friend who is also a manager, for advice.

Sandy suggests privately talking to Judy the next day. Even though Ted does not like the idea, he agrees.

Early the next morning, shortly after the branch opens, Ted asks Judy to come into his office. He begins: "Judy, I'm feeling like there's a real problem here. I know there's been a lot of discussion about my decision not to refund that woman's $15.00 service charge the other day. Now I can understand why people might disagree with it, but it is my decision to make. I can't have my employees second-guessing my decision, and I resent your talking with the customer about the decision the way you did. In the future—"

With the force of a dam bursting, Judy jumps into the middle of his sentence. She's already hot and angry. "What are you talking about?" she asks loudly and vehemently. "You don't know what I said to that customer! You don't have any proof!"

She catches her breath. Even more loudly, to the point of shouting, she continues: "You're always picking on me! The other day, you really embarrassed me in front of the other employees. You don't have the right to talk to me like this!"

Ted is speechless.

Judy draws her breath and vigorously stands up. "I don't have to listen to this. I'm going to quit!" She storms out of the office, picks up her purse at her desk, and walks out of the branch.

For a long time, Ted sits at his desk, stunned. When he finally walks into the lobby, the tension is almost unbearable. He tries to continue throughout the day, but his concentration is destroyed and his energy is drained.

103

CASE QUESTIONS

1. What went wrong? How should Ted have handled this discussion with Judy Miller?

2. Now that Judy has stormed out of the branch, what should he do...

   - with the staff that remains?
   - in notifying Human Resources?
   - with Judy Miller?

The Management Training Tool Kit: 35 Exercises to Prepare Managers for the Challenges They Face Every Day, ©2012 HRD Press.
Published by AMACOM Books, American Management Association, www.amanet.org.

Case Discussion:
Good News, Bad News: Part 3—The Storm Breaks

Summary: Part 3—The Storm Breaks

Acting on advice from a colleague, Ted meets with Judy the next morning. After a brief statement expressing his concerns, Judy explodes and accuses Ted of picking on her and embarrassing her. She quits and storms out of his office. Ted is stunned and the tension in the branch is almost unbearable.

Answers to Case Questions

1. **What went wrong? How should Ted have handled this discussion with Judy Miller?**

   If there was a problem, it may have been that Ted came across as a bit too confrontational and accusatory. Judy obviously was a powder keg ready to explode. Since this was the first meeting since events began deteriorating, Judy had been holding in a lot of pent-up feelings. Ted perhaps could have salvaged the meeting by using more assertive communication skills. He could have signaled his intentions more clearly at the outset.

   Example:

   "Judy, I need to talk with you about what's been going on in the branch recently. I have a feeling that you and some of the tellers are upset. I'd like to find out what's going on and what we need to do to fix it. I also realize that I may have made some mistakes. Can we talk about these matters openly and freely?"

2. **Now that Judy has stormed out of the branch, what should he do...**

   - **with the staff that remains?**
     Ted should hold a quick meeting with the staff to explain what happened and what will happen next.

   - **in notifying Human Resources?**
     Basically, the decision facing Ted at this point is whether to accept her resignation as is or to seek to retain her. Although it would be easy to let her quit, he should consider the alternative of keeping her. Judy is experiencing a lot of stress at this point, but she is a trained employee and, with help, she may be salvageable. This decision should be made in conjunction with Ted's boss or the next higher authority.

     Ted should notify Human Resources of the situation and the preferred course of action; that is, whether to accept her resignation or to put it on hold temporarily.

   - **with Judy Miller?**
     If the decision is to accept her resignation, Human Resources should send a letter to her confirming that action and notifying her of any final steps.

     If the decision is made to put her resignation on hold, she should be contacted by Human Resources (and not by Ted) to that effect. That is, a Human Resources officer should indicate that the bank recognizes the stress of the moment and would like to hold off taking final action for a period of time—a "cooling off period"—if Judy prefers.

105

Case 22 ✍

Conflict in Customer Service

Background Information

Brad Franklin had been supervising the Customer Service Unit of the Wilson chain of department stores for just over three years. The unit fulfilled an important function at Wilson: issuing company credit cards. Brad liked his job and was considered good at it. He had started as a credit analyst in the unit and, as a result of his hard work, did quite well. Now he was in charge of the unit's six credit analysts.

Almost half of all sales at Wilson were paid with Wilson credit cards, and there were always incoming applications. These applications, which had been completed by customers either at store locations or in response to mailings, went directly to the Customer Service Unit for credit analysis. The credit analysts did all the background information checking. They would identify credit references, double-check the accuracy of the information, and collect supporting information. Then, they would use the information to make a credit judgment. When an applicant qualified, the analysts would initiate a credit agreement and issue a credit card.

Because contracts and potential losses were involved, applications had to be handled carefully and precisely, and although the work was fairly routine, each application was unique. The job required an eye for detail, initiative, and skills in investigating and analyzing information. It also demanded a certain level of information needed for a credit judgment to be made, and it was not uncommon for both store managers and customers to call the unit to ask about the status of an application or account.

Although an employee could be trained to carry out these job requirements, Brad liked to hire candidates who already had some experience and, for quite some time, the credit analysts in his unit had all been young men with backgrounds in banking or financing. When two positions simultaneously opened up in the unit in March, Brad was faced with a potentially disastrous situation. Fortunately, he found two fairly good workers who both started their jobs on the same day. Because they were both trainees, he had them work together at adjacent desks. There they could work from the same files and could share the same phone.

One of the new employees, Don Fowler, 22, had been working with the Ace Finance Corporation for the previous nine months as an assistant credit investigator. He was very outgoing and hard working, and he soon fit in well with the other young men in the unit.

The other new employee was Karen Wilkens who, at age 20, had just completed an associate's degree at an area community college, with a specialty in business management. She was reserved and a bit shy. Even though she had no previous credit analysis experience, her work was very strong. Brad felt she had the potential to be a good analyst. If she felt uncomfortable about being the only woman in the unit, she kept it to herself.

107

Brad spent a lot of time training and working with both Don and Karen during their first two weeks on the job. He repeatedly showed them how to check references and carry out investigations. He always answered their questions and often told them to ask more questions if they were not sure what to do.

When Don and Karen finished their second week on the job, Brad told them to start answering phone calls about the applications and that he would still be available if they needed help. Since the phone was positioned between Don and Karen on their adjoining desk space, Brad expected them to alternate at this job, which entailed receiving the phone call, finding out the answers to the caller's questions, and then relaying the answers to the caller.

After a week or so, though, Brad began to notice something curious: Don always seemed to answer the phone. After he found out what the caller wanted, he would get up, look in the files, ask Brad questions, and take care of the call. Brad realized that he was now spending more time working with Don than with Karen and that Don was learning more because the phone calls led him into different types of investigations, thus broadening his knowledge. In Brad's estimation, Don was showing a lot of initiative and learning well.

But Brad also noticed that Don and Karen seemed to be arguing a lot. Their arguments were low-key enough to start with, but as the weeks progressed, they became more pointed and tense. Brad noted, too, how Karen often seemed to be angry and withdrawn: She never took part in the occasional joking among the unit's other men, nor did she join them on coffee breaks or for an after-hours drink.

Brad was particularly upset, though, when coaching Karen on investigations. He would try to talk with her, prefacing his comments with something like, "You remember when I taught you how to do this?" Karen would stop him and say, "You never trained me to do that, but you did train Don." Karen responded like this on a number of occasions.

There was no change in the situation until the last week of May, when Brad reviewed some work with Karen. Brad was mentioning how well Don had handled a similar application when Karen angrily interrupted him: "It's no wonder Don did so well! You trained him to do it and not me. You always spend time talking to him and never to me." Her voice grew bitter. "You didn't train me as well as you did him. And I think it's because I'm a woman." She pulled out a piece of paper from a file she was holding and shook it. "Look, I want to do a good job—and I have! I've been keeping a record of the investigations Don and I have done over the past two weeks. Look, I've been doing about five more each day than Don—he's always too busy talking on the phone and answering questions!"

Brad was shocked. That accusation, Brad believed, was very wrong. He knew that Karen's gender didn't make any difference to him: he had tried to help them both. He wasn't sure how to proceed.

The Management Training Tool Kit: 35 Exercises to Prepare Managers for the Challenges They Face Every Day, ©2012 HRD Press.
Published by AMACOM Books, American Management Association, www.amanet.org.

CASE QUESTIONS

1. What is the problem?

2. Are there any possible problems here for Brad under Equal Employment Opportunities laws?

3. Why would Karen react as she did?

4. What precautions might Brad have taken during the training process to avoid this problem?

5. How should Brad handle this problem?

The Management Training Tool Kit: 35 Exercises to Prepare Managers for the Challenges They Face Every Day, ©2012 HRD Press.
Published by AMACOM Books, American Management Association, www.amanet.org.

Case Discussion:
Conflict in Customer Service

Summary

Brad Franklin supervised the Customer Service Unit for the Wilson chain of department stores. When two positions in the unit opened up in March, Brad hired two new employees, Don and Karen. Don had some prior experience in this work, while Karen, who was a recent community college graduate, had none. She would be the only woman in the group.

Brad had them sit at adjacent desks for training and support reasons. He spent a lot of time training them during the first two weeks on the job. After two weeks, he instructed them to answer the phone and handle customer questions. Shortly thereafter, he noticed that Brad seemed to be doing more phone work than Karen. He also noticed that Brad and Karen seemed to argue a lot. Finally, Brad became concerned when Karen, a more shy and reserved person than Don, started to complain that she was not being trained as well as Don because she was a woman. Brad felt he was training them equally well and was surprised by Karen's remarks.

Answers to Case Questions

1. **What is the problem?**

   The problem here is Karen's perception and belief that she is being treated unfairly compared to a male peer, Don. Whether Brad has been treating her unfairly is not as important as the fact that Karen feels as if he has. His immediate problem is how to respond to this issue so that Karen can get beyond these feelings and become a fully functioning member of the team.

2. **Are there any possible problems here for Brad under Equal Employment Opportunities laws?**

   Yes, there could be a problem. Karen feels like she has been discriminated against in terms of a major condition of employment (training) because she is female. If she could "prove" that this discrimination did happen, Brad would be in violation of equal employment laws.

3. **Why would Karen react as she did?**

   It is generally unproductive to speculate on a person's motivation. However, there are two possible factors that may be at play here.

   First, Karen might be correct: whether wittingly or not, Brad may in fact have given her less adequate treatment than he did Don. If this turns out to be true, Brad will need to correct that problem immediately.

   Second, Karen may be feeling stress because of her unique status as a woman within the group. This feeling could tint her perceptions of how she is being treated. Again, the reason for her reaction is in general not as important as the need to address that feeling quickly and effectively.

   Concerning the issue of sexual harassment, there does not appear to be a problem in Brad's unit. There is no evidence of a sexually offensive environment here or of any expectation of sexual favors for work benefits.

4. **What precautions might Brad have taken during the training process to avoid this problem?**

Brad should have prepared a written training plan for both Don and Karen. Since they would both be doing the same job, the ultimate training results should be the same for each. However, since they came into the job with different backgrounds, they might start at different points. They would be expected to complete the training at different rates and speeds. This should have been explained to both during an orientation meeting. By noting check-off or completion stages on the training plan, Brad could have a record of the amount of training given to both. To review their progress, Brad should have established regular (weekly) review meetings with both Don and Karen, conducted on an individual basis.

Brad also should have given them specific phone coverage assignments. For example, Don might have been given the responsibility of handling all calls in the morning, and Karen all calls in the afternoon. Those schedules would have been rotated regularly.

As the only woman in the group, Karen may feel particularly vulnerable and under stress. Brad should have attended to her comfort level with the group of men. He should have resisted any pressures on her that might increase her discomfort level.

5. **How should Brad handle this problem?**

Brad should meet privately with Karen to discuss the matter. Brad should indicate that her concerns are very important to him and that he will do all he can to address them. He should also indicate that he had no intention of any differences in their training. Brad could also note, though, that Karen has to take some responsibility for her training, including initiative.

Brad should ask Karen to talk about the kinds of additional training she thinks she should receive. He should avoid talking with her about what in fact did happen and stay focused on what should happen in the future—going forward. The goal should be to produce a written training plan and a timetable that will keep him in regular contact with her and that will help her improve her skills.

Case 23 ✍

Don't Let an Old Flame Die

Background Information

Brenda Dawson worked hard, liked what she did, and was good at it. Brenda was the senior customer service associate trainer with American Products, Inc., a state-wide retail service organization with over 90 branch outlets. Typically, there were about four to six customer service associates (CSAs) in each branch office.

Brenda reported to Bill Abbott, head of the Training Department. Bill and Brenda started working in the Training Department at about the same time two years ago. Since then, Bill had noticed Brenda's natural talent for training. In his opinion, she had considerable potential for higher levels of responsibility, too—which was why he became concerned when Brenda started showing signs of becoming bored, stressful, and, in general, unenthusiastic about her work. Bill wanted to deal with the problem directly, but was not sure how to do it.

Late one day, after everyone had already left the offices, Bill took a break from a report on which he was working to recall some of the history and circumstances surrounding Brenda:

> Brenda was initially hired to work as a CSA and compiled a strong record of performance. After three years as a CSA, she was promoted to a position as a CSA supervisor in one of the busier branch offices. When the position of CSA trainer opened up, Brenda was a natural choice. She took over the CSA trainer job just a few months before Bill Abbott was hired. So when Bill moved in, Brenda was still learning the basics of training.

> During this period, American Products was undergoing a lot of changes itself, as it struggled to meet a variety of new competitive challenges in the marketplace. For example, in the boom economy of the time, CSA turnover was high. At one point, Brenda had to teach 12 people in classes that were designed for 8. And even with this 50 percent increase in training output, there was still a six-week waiting list to get into the training. Brenda would teach the class in the usual three-week period, take tests home at night to grade, use two days to finish up class records and order supplies, then get right back into the next class. When Bill finally received approval for a second trainer, Brenda had to train that person in addition to her hectic workload.

> Small wonder, Bill thought to himself, that she's ready to do something else.

He reviewed the current situation in his department. There were five people in the Training Department: in addition to Bill and Brenda, there was the second CSA trainer, Chris; a management trainee program coordinator; and the departmental secretary. All reported directly to Bill, who was now swamped with other projects.

113

Bill thought about what he wanted: fewer people reporting to him directly, a reinvigorated Brenda with new, more challenging assignments, and the entire CSA training effort coordinated and managed at a lower level.

As he sat staring out the window, absently toying with the pages of the report on which he was working, Bill made a list of some additional pieces to this puzzle:

1. Brenda had supervisory experience and the potential to supervise others. She already was serving in a senior, lead-worker capacity with Chris, the other CSA trainer.

2. Both Bill and Brenda were aware of the need for other CSA training programs. Some already existed, but could not be given because of time limitations, whereas others needed to be developed. For example, programs in customer relations, product knowledge, and sales skills had been "simmering on the back burner" for six months and were waiting for someone to put them together and deliver them.

3. The rate of CSA turnover was subsiding, and Bill knew that soon there would be a need for only one three-week CSA training class. This would cut out the need for running two classes at a time, as was done now.

4. There was a need for a new program for training CSA supervisors in branch service and supervisory tasks. This program would have to be developed.

5. Bill handled virtually all administrative and political issues in order to avoid burdening the staff. For example, the budgets for Brenda's CSA Training Center came directly to him each month, and Brenda never saw them. He did all the budget planning for her, too.

6. Likewise, Bill fielded all the problems and questions that the Branch Operations people had about CSA training. He had instituted the Advisory Committee of branch personnel to meet with the Training Department in order to act as a conduit for branch office complaints and to serve as a sounding board for departmental ideas. He knew this was a good approach. Brenda, while interested, said she'd never seen anything like that done before and claimed not to have time to get too involved.

7. Chris, the second CSA trainer, had been doing an acceptable job, but he needed help and coaching. Bill had neither the time nor the background to do that. Given these factors, Bill wondered what he could do to restructure Brenda's job in order to make it more challenging and satisfying while also improving the productivity and effectiveness of the department.

The Management Training Tool Kit: 35 Exercises to Prepare Managers for the Challenges They Face Every Day, ©2012 HRD Press.
Published by AMACOM Books, American Management Association, www.amanet.org.

CASE QUESTIONS

1. Is job enrichment an appropriate solution to this situation? If so, why?

2. Identify how you would redesign Brenda's job to enrich it. Write both a job description and a mission statement for Brenda's new job.

3. Identify how you would implement or go about completing this process. Think about how you would deal with the following: Brenda, Brenda's coworkers, other departmental staff, Branch Operations personnel, and the Personnel Department (for job evaluation). Create an implementation plan.

The Management Training Tool Kit: 35 Exercises to Prepare Managers for the Challenges They Face Every Day, ©2012 HRD Press.
Published by AMACOM Books, American Management Association, www.amanet.org.

Case Discussion:
Don't Let an Old Flame Die

Summary

Both Bill Abbott and Brenda Dawson moved into the Training Department at American Products, Inc., about the same time two years ago. American Products was a state-wide retail service organization of about 90 branch offices. One of the main activities of the Training Department was to train the customer service associates (CSAs) that staffed the branch offices. Bill headed the department, while Brenda was the senior CSA trainer.

Brenda started working at American Products as a CSA herself several years earlier. During that time, she proved to be a strong employee and had been promoted into a supervisory role within the branch. She was a natural choice for the CSA trainer's job when it opened. Once there, she worked very hard to keep up with the demand for training. Bill recognized that Brenda had some natural skills as a trainer and felt that she also had significant potential for further promotion. Recently, however, Bill had noticed that she was becoming "burned out," and he was quite concerned about what to do.

Bill surveyed some other characteristics of the situation. There was now a second CSA trainer in the department. This person needed more coaching and attention than Bill could provide. Brenda was already acting in a senior mentoring capacity with that person. There were also a variety of new training programs that were also in need of development. The rate of CSA turnover was subsiding; as a result, the demand for CSA classes had been cut in half. Bill handled all administrative matters for CSA training, such as budget preparation and review, program planning, and the like. He had started an Advisory Committee on the CSA training program, but Brenda said she had no knowledge or time to become involved with it.

Answers to Case Questions

1. Is job enrichment an appropriate solution to this situation? If so, why?

Yes. There are several reasons. First, Brenda is beginning to show signs of "demotivation" in the form of burnout; without some kind of response, Brenda may move on. Second, Brenda shows clear promise of development: learning new skills will help nurture those talents. Finally, Bill's ability to manage the department could improve by delegating more responsibility to Brenda.

2. Identify how you would redesign Brenda's job to enrich it. Write both a job description and a mission statement for Brenda's new job.

Under a job enrichment program, Brenda would move into a new job with higher levels of duties and responsibilities. The following duties are all candidates for her new job; these duties would be the core of any new job description.

Duties:

- Assuming full supervisory responsibility for the CSA trainer (Chris)
- Preparing and monitoring the budget for CSA training
- Designing and implementing additional CSA training programs as needed
- Leading the CSA Advisory Committee
- Providing backup CSA training as needed
- Managing (plan and evaluate) the CSA training and improving as indicated

The mission of this job would be to manage the CSA training function to provide quality training in a timely basis to all branch offices.

3. **Identify how you would implement or go about completing this process. Think about how you would deal with the following:**
   - **Brenda**—Bill should schedule a meeting with Brenda to express his interests in her career and well-being and to suggest a way to realize those interests through a job enrichment effort. He would explain how the initiative would work and enlist her involvement in the transition.

   - **Brenda's coworkers**—The biggest concern will be Chris, who is used to reporting to Bill directly. After the plans for Brenda's transition are underway, Bill should explain to Chris what the plans are and the new reporting relationships. This should include details of timing as well as listening to any concerns that Chris might have.

   - **Other departmental staff**—Bill should notify the rest of his staff accordingly.

   - **Branch Operations personnel**—The main customers of CSA training are the various personnel in the branch system, especially the operations managers. Bill should schedule a meeting with the key managers in that group to inform them of the news. Brenda should be at that meeting. This meeting would be a good opportunity to review the quality of service provided to date, identify any recurring problems, and develop common solutions to resolve those problems. Brenda should be the focus so that she will manage in response to these issues. Furthermore, Bill should expect to spend time with Brenda over the following months, coaching and helping her into this new management job.

   - **The Personnel Department**—Bill should notify Personnel that Brenda's job has been redesigned and that it needs to be regarded. Because of the higher levels of responsibility and skill required, Brenda should expect to receive a salary adjustment.

Create an implementation plan. Generally, the plan of implementation would be something like this:

1. Present the option to Brenda and enlist her agreement.
2. Begin developing a new job description and a plan for transferring duties. Notify Personnel.
3. Notify Chris and other employees in unit.
4. Begin coaching Brenda and preparing her for the transition.
5. Meet with Branch Operations and signal change.
6. Complete the transition; Bill continues to coach and support Brenda during the period.

Case 24 ✍

The Contradiction of Business

Background Information

First State Financial Services was the third largest banking institution in the state. It maintained an extensive branch and ATM network to service its diverse retail customer base. Even with First State's size, though, the business success of the bank was extremely dependent upon the trends in the local economy. Two years of recession meant two years of poor loans, and First State fell into deep trouble. To limit and reduce overhead expenses, there were some extensive layoffs. A new executive management expected rapid, better results with fewer resources. Everyone at First State feared being fired even though the bank was inching back to improved profitability. There was still the pressure to "perform—or else."

Lucy Winters managed the six-person Spring Hill Branch for First State. Spring Hill, fully equipped with an ATM and a freshly redesigned lobby, stood in the parking lot of a new suburban mall. The mall, anchored by a store from the largest grocery chain in the area, included about 20 different small retail stores. In addition, a major hospital was located just down the street, and a large manufacturing plant (with about 3,000 employees) was situated in a convenient, nearby industrial park. Many of the branch's customers worked at those locations.

Lucy was promoted to her current job about 18 months ago. She had been serving as an Assistant Manager at another branch in the region until that time. During the past year and a half, Lucy had learned her job as a manager well. She enjoyed her work and did an effective job.

"I *used* to enjoy it, in any case," she thought to herself. She was sitting at her desk at 6:00 p.m., looking at the night closing in. "I just wish I could leave here *once* before 5:30. These layoffs really hurt, the pressure is too great, and no one really cares whether I'm here or not." Lucy knew she was in a bad—no, depressed—mood.

The layoffs she was thinking about had taken place six months ago, but their full impact was only now being felt. Lucy's Spring Hill Branch was a busy one; previously there were nine positions authorized for it. Now there were only six: two New Accounts positions (including Lucy's) and four tellers. One teller could alternate between the teller line and back-office duties.

The problem was that there were too many customers. Lucy smiled at the contradiction: "Here the bank wants more customers, and we can't service the ones we already have." On almost any day at almost any time, there were three or four customers in line. It did not seem to matter that most of them simply wanted to cash a check or make a deposit: by the time they got to the teller, they were curt or rude, demanding, and sometimes hostile and aggressive.

Lucy clearly remembered an incident that had occurred just two days ago. A customer had been waiting for about 20 minutes to pay a bill. When he finally reached the window, he started berating the tellers for being so slow and condemning the bank for being so inept. By the time he finished, the teller was in tears.

119

Lucy remembered talking to her after he left. The teller said, "We work so hard and no one seems to appreciate what we do. I just can't work like this."

Lucy started to hear a lot more complaints—from everybody, it seemed. Customers complained about poor service, the tellers were complaining about the pressure, and "downtown" was starting to complain about the large number of mistakes, errors, and shortages being made at the branch.

Tomorrow Lucy had to hold one of her monthly sales meetings with the staff. These meetings were required by "downtown." Lucy dreaded them because they always seemed to drag on and on and nothing ever got accomplished. Lucy was supposed to talk about a product for 15 to 20 minutes or so, and she could envision everyone else sitting there, fidgeting in their seats or looking at the floor. There would be no questions, but there would be occasional complaints about how "we need more help" or "the customers are yelling at us."

Lucy was not looking forward to tomorrow's meeting and wondered if there were ways she could work on the real problems in the branch and produce real results from her meeting.

CASE QUESTIONS

1. Can Lucy use this meeting to help solve some of the problems at the branch?

2. What kinds of general strategies can Lucy pursue to help solve these problems?

3. Describe the process that Lucy can follow with her staff to address productivity and quality problems.

The Management Training Tool Kit: 35 Exercises to Prepare Managers for the Challenges They Face Every Day, ©2012 HRD Press.
Published by AMACOM Books, American Management Association, www.amanet.org.

Case Discussion:
The Contradiction of Business

Summary

Lucy Winters managed a branch bank office. The office was located in a good location and had many customers. However, the bank itself had been under severe pressure to improve profits. As a result, the staff in Lucy's office had been reduced by a third.

Now there seemed to be a constant backup of customers in the branch. Because of long waits, customers were often abusive to the tellers when they finally reached the window. The staff was feeling increasingly stressful, and the quality of work began falling off.

The contradiction of this business was that, as things stood now, Lucy had more customers than she was capable of handling.

Two days after a particularly disturbing incident, Lucy prepared to conduct a mandated "sales meeting" in the branch. These meetings seldom went well as far as Lucy was concerned. She wanted to find some way to deal with the real problems of the branch, and felt she had to come up with something before the meeting on the following day.

Answers to Case Questions

1. **Can Lucy use this meeting to help solve some of the problems at the branch?**

   Absolutely. But it is very likely that it will take a series of meetings with the staff to dig a way out of these problems.

   The basic problem is that the current configuration of staffing and customers is out of balance: the demand for services exceeds the staff's ability to serve the customers. The key to improving the productivity of the branch is to reconfigure the service and customer mix.

2. **What kinds of general strategies can Lucy pursue to help solve these problems?**

   Lucy has several options that she can pursue to help solve this problem.

   First, she can request additional staff from her management. Along with asking for full-time workers, she could suggest a number of options such, as part-time positions or sharing staff with another branch. She could even pursue the latter option on her own initiative with friendly peer branch managers.

   Second, part of the productivity problem involves customers using tellers for transactions that could be completed through other more efficient channels. There are several ways that customers could be approached and encouraged to use more productive methods, such as direct deposit of payroll checks and use of automatic teller machines (ATMs) and online banking and bill paying options. Since her branch is near a number of employers, she could recommend a marketing strategy to contact these employers for the purpose of establishing direct payroll deposit. She could also work with Marketing to create in-branch promotional campaigns to increase ATM usage banking.

   Third, she needs to work with her staff to find ways to improve service. This latter approach would involve the staff in looking for recurring problems and appropriate solutions to them.

3. Describe the process that Lucy can follow with her staff to address productivity and quality problems.

Basically, Lucy should launch a quality circle or productivity improvement initiative with her staff. There are several major steps involved in implementing such an initiative:

1. She needs to explain the program to her staff members and indicate that this is one way they can try to improve their situation. She could indicate some of the things she is already trying (see answer to Question 2). She should indicate that this process will be an ongoing one.

2. She should obtain training for her and her staff in quality and productivity improvement techniques. She should also develop the practice of providing performance reports to the staff.

3. She should use regular meetings to identify problems and brainstorm solutions.

4. Part of her actions should be to improve the training of her staff. This can occur in two areas: dealing with difficult customers and technical areas of branch work. She would need to seek training support for these areas.

Case 25 ✎

Problems Behind the Counter

Background Information

Bob Cramer, 36 and recently divorced, manages the Oak Street Branch for the Second National Bank and Trust. The Oak Street Branch has six tellers and does an average amount of business. Bob has been with Second National since he graduated from college, when he joined the management training program. Bob is well liked and generally enjoys his job, although now, at the height of summer, he is carrying out the difficult job of preparing a disciplinary warning for one of his staff members.

Eight months ago, in January, Bob hired a new teller by the name of Connie Tremont. Connie was 23 years old and a graduate of a local high school. Connie had experience working as a claims clerk with an insurance company prior to coming to Second National. Bob spent about 15 minutes interviewing her and, although he had a few reservations about her appearance and communication manner, he desperately needed someone who could start soon, and she was available immediately. Bob decided to take a chance.

She started in Second Bank's three-week teller training school the next Monday and finished it successfully. On her first day at the Oak Street Branch, Bob gave her his standard five-minute welcome, then turned her over to the head teller. The head teller introduced her to the other tellers, helped her get set up, told her to ask if she had any questions, and then went back to her job. Connie began serving customers soon thereafter.

Like all new tellers, it took her a long time to get adjusted and settled in. During these break-in periods, Bob would wonder whether the teller training was really needed because it always seemed to him that the tellers forgot everything once they walked in the door. Nonetheless, he noticed that in spite of these difficulties, Connie picked up the essentials of her work and began performing at an acceptable level relatively quickly.

Unfortunately, Bob was also finding that the initial concerns he had about Connie during the interview process had been well founded. While she could complete the technical aspects of her work acceptably, she had a major problem with presenting herself to, and working favorably with, the bank's customers. Bob wondered almost daily when she would recognize this problem and do something about it, but she seemed oblivious to the matter and simply would not change. After six months, Bob knew that if she did not come around quickly, he would have no other choice but to release her. Although he dreaded the thought of being short-staffed again, he thought to himself, "I've been short-staffed so many times before that I should be used to it."

Connie's major problem is really a result of several factors. One factor is her physical appearance: she is pretty and slightly overweight, but pleasingly so. Unfortunately, she is obviously inattentive to grooming and personal hygiene—and Bob does not hae any sympathy for poor, sloppy grooming. After seeing repeated examples of her neglect,

The Management Training Tool Kit: 35 Exercises to Prepare Managers for the Challenges They Face Every Day, ©2012 HRD Press.
Published by AMACOM Books, American Management Association, www.amanet.org.

Bob has been forced to conclude that she is simply a slob. Her long hair is frequently disheveled and uncombed; it often seems to be unwashed. Her style of dress is plainly inappropriate, too: she often wears clothes that are either too loose and low-cut, or too tight and revealing.

Over the past eight months, a number of incidents related to Connie's poor grooming habits have occurred. Bob could easily recall an incident that happened three weeks ago on July 18 when the branch was filled with a lunch crowd. Bob, standing near the front of the teller counter with a customer, saw Connie bend over to get some supplies from under the counter. Her dress hiked up substantially, revealing her upper legs and underwear. He saw that many of the customers had noticed, too, and were looking away in embarrassment.

Bob knew that this kind of image was not acceptable for the kind of business establishment he was expected to run. He talked with her privately the next day and told her what had happened, why it was a problem, and that she must be careful. However, in the days and weeks that followed, he detected no changes in her grooming or hygiene.

Another reason for her customer contact problem is her poor manner of communicating with customers: she is often just plain rude. Bob has regularly heard her argue with customers in a loud and contentious voice, at times cutting them off rather abruptly. It is as if she has a chip on her shoulder and almost anything a customer might do will knock it off.

Bob has received frequent complaints from customers regarding her abrasive behavior. For example, last Monday, August 2, when a customer asked to borrow a pen, Bob overheard her tell him, "Well, I don't like to give up my pen because whenever I do, customers always keep it. Be sure to give it back to me." He called her to his office as soon as the customer left and admonished her about what she did and told her she had better improve her conduct.

Bob was reaching a point of decision. The last straw occurred yesterday, Thursday, August 5, over Bob's "no barefooting it" rule. The background to the problem is that many tellers take off their shoes, especially toward the end of the day, in order to be more comfortable. Usually this poses no problem. However, throughout the summer, Bob received a growing number of complaints from the tellers that Connie's feet and shoes smelled terrible. Two days ago, on Wednesday afternoon, Bob personally verified the problem. Yesterday, before the bank opened, he told the tellers that they should keep their shoes on.

Not an hour later, Bob was amazed to find Connie barefoot. He told her to put her shoes on. Later in the afternoon, he again found her barefoot, but this time he decided to give her a written warning notice. In the bank's disciplinary procedure, issuing such a warning is the last major step before termination. Unless there was clear and immediate improvement after Connie received the notice, Bob intended to fire her.

Now, on Friday morning, Bob reads over the following rules for completing a written warning notice in the bank's policy and procedures manual:

The Management Training Tool Kit: 35 Exercises to Prepare Managers for the Challenges They Face Every Day, ©2012 HRD Press.
Published by AMACOM Books, American Management Association, www.amanet.org.

- The expected standards for performance must be stated.

- Specific examples (with dates, times, locations, examples) of the offending behavior must be identified.

- A deadline for improvement must be set.

- The employee should sign the form, or if he or she refuses, a note to that effect must be added. The employee may add remarks to the document. The employee keeps a copy, with the original sent to Personnel for filing in the employee's folder. It is kept for two years and removed from the folder if there have been no other problems during that time.

He picks up his pen and gets to work, aware that he will be discussing the warning's content with Connie later in the day after she receives it.

ASSIGNMENT

Given the information presented in this case and using the form provided, prepare a written warning notice. Use this form to conduct a role play with someone who plays "Connie."

Note: Connie writes the following comment on the form when Bob gives it to her:

My boss Bob Cramer is a real jerk. He picks on me and upsets me. I would do a much better job if I worked for a good boss. I want a transfer.

Case Conclusion

After the discussion is completed, Connie signs the form and is handed a copy. As she starts to walk from Bob's office, she tears it up into little pieces and throws it on his desk.

CASE QUESTION

What should Bob do now?

125

Second National Bank
Written Warning Notice

Employee name: _____

Department/Branch: _____ Date: _____

This warning is to notify you that you are not meeting minimal acceptable standards of performance for your job. Continued performance below standard may result in your termination. Immediate improvement is needed to avoid further disciplinary action.

Standard of performance: _____

_____

_____

Example(s) of inadequate performance: _____

_____

_____

_____

_____

Improvements needed: _____

_____

_____

_____

_____

Prior notice of problem to employee: ❑ Verbal   ❑ Written

Date: _____

Employee remarks: _____

_____

_____

_____

Signatures:

_____   _____
Manager   Employee

126

Case Discussion:
Problems Behind the Counter

Summary

Bob Cramer managed a branch bank office and was experiencing problems with a staff member. Eight months ago, he filled an open teller's position with Connie Tremont. Connie, 23, had been working as a claims clerk since graduating from a local high school. Bob spent 15 minutes interviewing her for the job. Although he had some reservations about her, he needed the help. She began the bank's training program the next week. Upon finishing the program, she returned to the branch. Bob welcomed her and then his head teller gave Connie a quick orientation and setup, after which time she began serving customers.

After a month or so, it became clear to Bob that his initial concerns about Connie were well grounded. Connie had pronounced problems with making a favorable impression on customers. There were several ways in which these problems manifested themselves—and are still manifesting themselves. One issue is poor personal hygiene and grooming. A second is the inappropriate style of clothing she wears to work. A third issue is her rudeness to customers. He has started receiving complaints from customers although he had informally counseled her about improving her performance in these matters several times before.

A "final straw" occurred yesterday. After receiving some complaints from the other tellers about Connie's foot odor, Bob ordered the tellers to keep their shoes on. On two different occasions that day, Bob found her disobeying his directive. Now he is ready to issue her a written warning notice, the last step before termination in the bank's disciplinary policy. He has a copy of the procedures.

Assignment

> **Given the information presented in this case and using the form provided, prepare a written warning notice. Use this form to conduct a role-play with someone who plays "Connie."**

Note: Connie writes the following comment on the form when Bob gives it to her: *My boss Bob Cramer is a real jerk. He picks on me and upsets me. I would do a much better job if I worked for a good boss. I want a transfer.*

Employees have the right to make whatever comments they please on the form. Even though this comment is inflammatory, Bob cannot have it removed. Bob could tell Connie, though, that she will need his recommendation for any transfer and that she needs to improve no matter what she thinks of him personally.

Answer to Case Question

What should Bob do now?

After the discussion is completed, Connie signs the form and is handed a copy. As she starts to walk from Bob's office, she tears it up into little pieces and throws it on his desk. If Connie did this act in full view of other employees, her behavior could be considered gross insubordination and could be grounds for immediate dismissal.

If it was done in private, Bob has two options:

1. He could just ignore it.

2. He could take further action

The first option, while no doubt difficult to do, might be indicated if she was particularly upset. However, he could instruct her to return and pick up the material for disposal in the wastepaper basket. In and of itself, the document was her copy to do with as she pleased, and there was nothing inherently wrong in tearing up the document. The offense would be in throwing it on his desk rather than in the garbage.

Given the symbolic nature of her action, though, a stronger response is needed. In this context, he could call her back into his office and issue yet another notice, this time for insubordination, including a clause about grounds for immediate termination for any future insubordinate acts of this kind.

Case 26 ✍️

Wanted: Good Secretary

Background Information

For over three years, Bernard Malinowski had been the manager of the Customer Service Department at Buford Department Store. After nearly six years working in various customer service assignments, he still enjoyed the work of responding to the inquiries, requests, and complaints of Buford's various retail customers. He felt it was a way to help the customers and Buford at the same time.

He supervised five service representatives who dealt directly with the customers. At times, the service representatives would also support different marketing programs and initiatives. There was one secretary for the department who provided the administrative and clerical support needed to keep the department running efficiently. Bernard realized all too well how important it was to have a top performer in that position.

That was why he was so concerned—and surprised—by the recent performance of his new secretary, Betty Lyons. Bernard's expectations had been high when he hired Betty two months ago. He thought she would be the one who might stick around and solve the "revolving door" problem he had experienced with every former occupant of that job. But now, he started to think about replacing Betty.

When she started in Customer Service, Betty seemed to be the ideal worker: she was energetic, cared about doing a good job, worked hard, and got along well with her coworkers. But here she was, making the same old mistakes all her predecessors had made. He ticked off in his own mind the now familiar list of problems:

- Letters to customers always looked sloppy and poorly composed. The recent addition of word processing software to the computer in the unit had not resulted in any improvements.

- The turnaround time for producing the letters was too long, often seeming to take two or three days from the date of submission.

- Filing and recordkeeping duties piled up and never seemed to be completed on any sort of timely or up-to-date basis.

To make matters worse, recently she had started complaining of being "overworked." Indeed, Bernard overheard her say to one of the service representatives just yesterday, "Have they ever told you what they expect you to do or what the priorities are around here? I'm so busy and pulled in so many directions, I can't do everything. And I don't know what I'm supposed to do first."

Bernard knew she was not performing up to standard and that he would have to act soon. He thought to himself: "It's funny, but the good ones always seem to have the most problems. When they do their work well, we give them more to do, and then bang—their work falls to pieces. The mediocre ones always stay mediocre—just getting the job barely done." Bernard felt the people should derive satisfaction

129

from completing a job done well—and if not, well, he did give them a pay raise once a year. "That should be reward enough," he thought.

And that was all the reward he gave them.

CASE QUESTIONS

1. Is there a performance problem?

2. Describe the issues.

3. How should Bernard respond?

The Management Training Tool Kit: 35 Exercises to Prepare Managers for the Challenges They Face Every Day, ©2012 HRD Press.
Published by AMACOM Books, American Management Association, www.amanet.org.

Case Discussion:
Wanted: Good Secretary

Summary

Bernard Malinowski supervised the five service representatives and one secretary in the Customer Service Department at Buford Department Store. The secretarial position provided important support to all the service representatives. There had been a steady turnover of personnel in this position. When Bernard hired Betty Lyons two months ago, he thought things might be different. At first, they were; he was actually pleased with her work.

However, he was now concerned about her performance: letters looked sloppy, correspondence took too long to get out, and filing and recordkeeping were behind schedule. Moreover, Betty was complaining about being overworked and not having any direction. Bernard thought that he might need to terminate her if things didn't improve.

Bernard believed that the good employees always seemed to be the most disappointing. They did well, were given more work, and then their performance failed. He believed annual merit raises were sufficient rewards for good work, and that was the only kind of reinforcement he gave them.

Answers to Case Questions

1. Is there a performance problem?

Yes. There is a problem with Betty's work output and quality. There is also a problem with the staffing of the secretarial position: high levels of turnover in a position indicate problems in the management of that position.

2. Describe the issues.

There is a quality (and productivity) problem with certain aspects of Betty's job. Presumably, these problems arose after an initially successful period of job performance. There is evidence, then, that she can technically perform the job under certain conditions.

However, it appears that those conditions have changed: she has been given an excessive workload without any corresponding sense of priorities or appreciation for the work she has done. It also appears that she has received inadequate training.

Although not described in the case, it is reasonable to suppose that the frequent turnover of personnel in this position may be due to the same underlying causes. And those causes come back to Bernard's inadequate efforts to manage the position and the person in that position.

3. How should Bernard respond?

Bernard has two matters to which he must attend. First, he needs to work on the immediate problems of Betty's performance. Second, he needs to manage the position more effectively in order to remove the underlying reasons for poor performance.

On the first point, Bernard should meet with Betty to identify the exact production problems she is facing. It is likely that he will need to do the following with her:

- Provide additional training
- Identify priorities
- Reinforce good performance
- Give her some temporary support to clear out any backlog of work

Second, he needs to manage the position. This means looking at the work done in the position and determining whether there are more productive and efficient ways to do it. He should seriously look into ways to reduce the workload or, if that option is not possible, to find ways to do the job more easily. Part of this effort can be done cooperatively and participatively with Betty, and perhaps with the full staff, as part of an "employee involvement" productivity improvement. Modeled along the lines of a quality circle, he could schedule a series of meetings with the staff to look for ways to reduce the nature of the problems.

Case 27 ✍

Another Staff Meeting

Background Information

June Hanks had worked for Jim McLin for almost one year now, but she still was not used to these last-minute staff meetings. It was difficult to predict when they would occur. Some meetings might come within days of each other, whereas other meetings might be months apart. No matter when they were scheduled, though, she could count on one thing: they would be set up at the last minute. June knew that most of the other six managers in the department who also attended these meetings felt the same way she did: Jim's supervisory style could be somewhat frustrating.

Although not yet accustomed to Jim's last-minute meetings, June was not particularly surprised to learn that a meeting had suddenly been scheduled for that afternoon at 3:30. She asked Rudy Bronstein, the coworker who told her about the meeting, what it was about. Rudy just shrugged his shoulders as if to say "Who knows?"

Jim's staff were assembled in the meeting room at 3:30. As was common, Jim arrived about 10 minutes late, apologizing profusely. As he settled into his chair, he said, "It's been a while since our last meeting, and I felt like we all needed a chance to catch up on what was going on in the department and throughout the rest of the company."

June caught Rudy's attention and rolled her eyes. All of their meetings started like this, she thought, and they usually led nowhere. She soon discovered, however, that this meeting would be different.

After going around the table and obtaining a brief report from each of his staff members, Jim announced: "We have got to take care of this red-tape problem."

He paused as if to let the message sink in, but there was nothing shocking about it. Since the first day June worked for Jim, she had heard him complain that his department spent too much time on "red tape"—his code word for a lot of detailed procedures that he felt people followed too closely. Jim liked to expand on this topic at every occasion, although almost everyone else felt there was no effective way to reduce or cut out the variety of organizationally required forms and procedures they had to complete. June felt like telling him that there were far more important issues to focus on.

"I'm really serious about it this time," Jim continued. "I want each of you to bring me at least three ideas for how we can cut down on the red tape we have here. I'll expect them in writing on my desk first thing tomorrow morning."

June could not hold her tongue any longer: "Jim, that's a very difficult task to complete. I was planning to work late tonight on that Howard project you assigned me last week. I just can't do them both. Besides, if we have an urgent problem to take care of, it's this new VIP service program. It's causing a lot of problems for everyone at this table."

133

The VIP service program was an initiative Jim had begun a few months ago. The intent of the program was honorable: to provide the best service possible. However, in practice, the program was a nightmare. It obligated everyone in the department to stop whatever they were doing in order to fix a problem of any magnitude. Jim did not see the need for addressing why the problems occurred to begin with or trying to distinguish major from minor problems. As a result, his staff members had their work interrupted more frequently, which in turn led to more errors in their ongoing work. June knew that all of her coworkers had been complaining about these problems, and she noticed supportive smiles and nods from others around the table.

Jim paused for a minute, looking at June. He then said, "June, you know that you haven't had that much experience with this program yet, and besides, I know that what you'd propose can't be done and wouldn't work anyway. No, let's stick with the red-tape problem."

Jim looked around the group. "Now, let's see what else is going on. Who'd like to share any further ideas or suggestions?" There were no volunteers, and Jim had to do some considerable coaxing to receive any additional comments.

He finally ended the meeting after 15 minutes of forced, half-hearted discussion. Everyone left quickly without saying a word to him.

CASE QUESTION

Evaluate how well Jim managed this meeting. What could he have done differently to make it more productive?

The Management Training Tool Kit: 35 Exercises to Prepare Managers for the Challenges They Face Every Day, ©2012 HRD Press.
Published by AMACOM Books, American Management Association, www.amanet.org.

Case Discussion:
Another Staff Meeting

Summary

Jim McLin called staff meetings on the spur of the moment. His staff could not predict when these meetings would occur or what the meetings would cover. Sure enough, June Hanks just learned that there would be such a meeting at 3:30 today.

As usual, Jim arrived about 10 minutes late. He began by asking for any general catch-up information. After everyone spoke for a few minutes, he brought up a subject that he frequently talked about: the departmental red-tape problem. In Jim's opinion, the department spent too much time on red-tape procedures. He said he really wanted to do something about it this time and told everyone to submit at least three suggestions to him first thing the following morning.

June Hanks spoke up, pointing out that if they had a real issue to address, it was Jim's VIP program. Jim had installed this program a few months ago to improve service. Under this program, his employees were expected to drop whatever they were doing whenever a problem developed and to fix the problem before resuming their work. In practice, this program was creating more problems than it was solving. Jim refused to discuss it. He tried to move on to other matters, but after no success, the meeting was adjourned. Everyone left quickly.

Answer to Case Question

Evaluate how well Jim managed this meeting. What could he have done differently to make it more productive?

Jim did a generally poor job of managing this meeting process. Staff members were given a chance to talk briefly about what was going on in their units, but otherwise, the meeting could not be judged a success. First, Jim did not give his employees time to prepare. Second, he forced a response to a situation that had no apparent sense of urgency. Third, he did not encourage a frank discussion of his employees' concerns. Finally, he created a climate that inhibited a full discussion of employee concerns.

In short, whether by design or by accident, Jim operated as if according to a "hidden agenda," and it seemed he was not open to changing this agenda for any reason, not even to respond to valid employee concerns. However, the primary purpose of a meeting like this should be to facilitate the free flow of information and thus improve the performance of all concerned, and in this respect, the meeting was a failure.

There are several steps Jim could take to improve his meeting management skills:

1. *Commit to a regular schedule of meetings.*
   By scheduling meetings at the last minute, Jim is signaling the low priority these meetings have for him. While it is not imperative for him to establish a regular meeting time (such as every Monday at 9:00 a.m.), he should at least conclude each meeting by scheduling the next meeting on a specific date and within a reasonable period of time.

2. *Empower the team members to call meetings on their own.*
   Jim has tended to allow his staff members to become passive in this area. He should give them the authority to call meetings even if he is unavailable.

3. *Prepare an agenda of items that should be covered in the meeting.*
   Jim should distribute the agenda to staff members in advance of the meeting. He should flag any items that require staff preparation and provide them with any necessary reference materials.

4. *When the meeting begins, ask if anyone wishes to add to the agenda.*
   By involving staff members in this way, Jim would update his knowledge of problems they were experiencing and stay abreast of the resurgence of any former problems that he had considered resolved. He also indirectly conveys to his staff members that their input is important to him and that each of them is a vital member of the team.

5. *Budget time for each agenda item and inform staff of the desired resolution of the discussion.*
   For example, if Jim wants to discuss a certain problem, he should indicate that the desired resolution of the discussion is a problem statement with someone designated in charge of further researching it.

6. *Respond constructively to participant remarks. Encourage open, and even dissenting, views rather than discouraging them.*
   In this particular meeting, Jim's reaction to June's comments about the VIP program essentially shut down the conversation. In cases like this, he should have asked the other staff members if this was an important issue to discuss. If they answered yes, he could have solicited their opinions and suggestions. If only some members were interested or there was no time to pursue the matter, he could have tabled the discussion until the next meeting or have spoken to staff members independent of any meeting.

7. *Use the meeting to brainstorm ideas about the problem rather than asking participants to complete a separate assignment on the problem.*
   Jim could have used this method to address the red-tape problem. In general, he should improve his basic group problem-solving skills and use them more effectively.

8. *Take time to consider why the meetings are held and whether there is a better alternative.*
   For example, if Jim's idea is simply to get his subordinate managers together regularly to exchange information about their projects, he should ask how critical that information is and whether there might be easier ways to exchange that information.

Case 28 ✍

The Case-in-Case Analysis

Background Information

Jerry Brown, 42, was promoted to supervisor of the Case Analysis Unit just three months ago. The Case Analysis Unit was a special investigation group within the city's Department of Social Services. The four employees in this unit investigated suspected fraud cases and researched various special requests for exemptions and services.

The investigations conducted by the case analysis representatives typically began by verifying data obtained from applicants during the intake process. Then, field agents as well as employers or claimants would be contacted as necessary for additional information. The information gathered from all these sources would be reviewed, and a recommendation for either "no further action" or "prosecution" would be issued. While the unit's workload fluctuated somewhat, the average standard of production was 12 completed cases per week and 4 backlogged cases cleared.

Jerry believed that everyone in his unit was doing an acceptable job except Frank Harrison. Frank, 46, had been with the department for 22 years, the last eight of which were spent in this unit. Frank's usual rate of performance was 7 cases a week, with 1 or 2 backlogged cases cleared.

Jerry remembered a conversation with Sullivan Hart, the previous supervisor of this unit, whose retirement had opened up the supervisory opportunity for Jerry. The conversation took place about four months before Sullivan's last scheduled day, when they were having lunch together. Jerry had just been named as Sullivan's replacement, and they were discussing different aspects of the transition and the operations of the Case Analysis Unit.

Jerry remembered Sullivan's remarks very clearly: "Frank just doesn't have the motivation to do an adequate job and, to be honest with you, I'm too close to retirement to rock the boat."

Sullivan had paused, putting down his fork.

"You know," he continued, "I finally got to the point with Frank that I'd be pleased if I got 7 or 8 completed cases from him each week. Everyone else ended up taking up the slack."

After that conversation, Jerry began to watch Frank more closely. Sure enough, Frank seemed to move more slowly, stop more often, put aside more challenging tasks, and ask for help more frequently than his coworkers in the unit. Otherwise, though, Frank was a model employee. He was seldom absent and arrived at work on time every day. The quality of his work was almost as good as the work done by the other employees. He was polite and considerate, even if he did not socialize as freely as the others did.

Jerry looked in Frank's personnel folder. He found no record of any previous counseling or disciplinary procedures, but did find Frank's most recent performance appraisal, which had been conducted by Sullivan Hart about a month before he left. Jerry was disturbed but not surprised by what he saw: Sullivan had rated Frank as

The Management Training Tool Kit: 35 Exercises to Prepare Managers for the Challenges They Face Every Day, ©2012 HRD Press.
Published by AMACOM Books, American Management Association, www.amanet.org.

an "above-average" employee (a 4 on a scale of 5). According to Sullivan, Frank's productivity was in line with the unit's standards. He had written: "Frank does his job well and has a long history of good performance with the city." There was no indication in the appraisal or in the file that there had ever been a notice given to Frank about work standards or a discussion with him about how he could improve his work performance.

Under the city's merit review system, the higher the evaluation rating, the larger the salary increase an employee was entitled to. For example, employees rated as doing an acceptable job would receive an average increase of about 4 percent; those rated above average, 6 percent; and those rated superior, 8 percent. Sure enough, Frank's salary had been adjusted by about 5.5 percent as a result of this last review.

Jerry was learning about another problem related to Frank's performance. Shortly after assuming the supervisor's job, Jerry began sensing how much anger and hostility the other employees in the unit had toward Frank. At first, he would overhear side comments directed at Frank during meetings or discussions, but recently he had noticed that Frank's coworkers were making these comments more openly. For example, in a recent staff meeting, an initial joke about how slowly an applicant responded to a fraud claim was compared to Jerry's processing of cases. While he sat there, obviously uncomfortable, the others ridiculed him contemptuously. Before Jerry could regain order, there was a lot of psychological "blood" on the floor.

As a result of that episode, Jerry became concerned about the long-term effects this situation would have on the morale and performance of the unit if he let the situation continue.

CASE QUESTIONS

1. Describe the problem(s) that Jerry is facing.

2. Should Jerry do anything about the less-than-standard performance of Frank Harrison? If so, what should his performance management strategy be?

3. What should Jerry do about Frank in relation to the other employees in the unit?

The Management Training Tool Kit: 35 Exercises to Prepare Managers for the Challenges They Face Every Day, ©2012 HRD Press.
Published by AMACOM Books, American Management Association, www.amanet.org.

Case Discussion:
The Case-in-Case Analysis

Summary

Jerry Brown was made supervisor of the Case Analysis Unit of the city's Department of Social Services about three months ago. There were four employees in the unit. They were expected to complete 12 cases and clear 4 backlogged cases each week.

Jerry was pleased with every employee except Frank Harrison. Frank was a long-term city employee who had been in this unit for the past eight years. Frank was polite and likeable, but his usual level of performance was 7 cases and 1 or 2 backlogged cases weekly. After watching Frank's work more closely, Jerry observed that Frank worked more slowly than his coworkers.

Before Jerry's predecessor and boss, Sullivan Hart, retired, he told Jerry that Frank just lacked motivation. However, his boss also said that he didn't want to rock the boat over Frank. Sure enough, when Jerry finally looked in Frank's personnel folder, he noticed that no counseling or disciplinary actions had been recorded and found that Frank had been given generally good performance appraisals. Frank was given a better-than-average merit pay increase the month before Jerry took over as supervisor.

Jerry also noticed how the other employees began to disparage and make fun of Frank. During one meeting at which he was present, they openly ridiculed him before Jerry could regain control of the situation. Jerry became concerned about the long-term effects Frank would have on the morale of the unit.

Answers to Case Questions

1. **Describe the problem(s) that Jerry is facing.**

   Jerry is facing two immediate problems. These two problems are related. Furthermore, by dealing with these problems, Jerry could face a third problem. The two immediate problems are (1) Frank's less-than-satisfactory performance and (2) the dissension this poor performance is creating among the other employees. Given Frank's age, if Jerry begins to take action and is not careful, he could run into accusations of age discrimination.

2. **Should Jerry do anything about the less-than-standard performance of Frank Harrison? If so, what should his performance management strategy be?**

   Yes, Jerry should take action for two reasons. First, the productivity of his unit is suffering because of Frank's slow performance, which in turn is reducing the quality of service provided by the unit. Second, Frank's poor performance is triggering problems among other employees, which could generate an even more serious problem.

   To manage this situation, Jerry should first create a record of Frank's performance in terms of the typical performance of the unit. Even if he goes back for just a few months, Jerry can clearly demonstrate how poorly Frank's performance measures up. Second, once a clear pattern is graphed, he should meet with Frank. The purpose of this meeting is not punitive; rather, it is to begin a discussion of the issues.

In the meeting, Jerry should state that he needs to talk with Frank and get the issue on the table, that this is an informal meeting, and that no adverse actions toward Frank will result from the meeting. Jerry should explain why Frank's performance is a concern, then ask for Frank's feedback. They can discuss ways to overcome the problem, such as Jerry keeping a weekly record he would share with Frank. Jerry should ask whether Frank needs training and coaching, then provide it if necessary. Frank's ideas on how to improve his performance should be requested and discussed. Jerry should also make it clear in writing what the acceptable standards of performance are and how Frank will be rated next year if his current level of performance continued. Later, he should make a note of this meeting and keep it in a file apart from Frank's personnel record.

If Frank's performance does not improve, Jerry should be ready to move into a more formal counseling mode with Frank. During these discussions, Jerry could raise the issue of career placement with Frank: if Frank is not performing this task well, perhaps it is time for him to think of moving to another position. Or, if circumstances permit, Jerry might redesign Frank's job to make it easier to do—and seek a re-grading downward.

Given Frank's age-protected status, Jerry should be in close consultation with the Human Resources Department and should be keeping good notes on discussions with Frank and actions taken.

If none of these tactics work, Jerry may be forced to terminate Frank's employment.

3. What should Jerry do about Frank in relation to the other employees in the unit?

This is a tough position. It would be inadvisable for Jerry to say anything about Frank and his counseling to others in the unit because there is a chance this could lead to defamation problems. On the other hand, he could assure them that there will be improvements in matters, one way or another, and that Jerry does not want to hear backbiting comments during their meetings. He could also encourage the employees to offer support.

Case 29 ✍

A "No" in the Field

Background Information

Marjorie Brown supervised the Northwood local office of Helping Hand, Inc. Helping Hand was a nonprofit private service agency that provided transportation and housing services to people throughout the metropolitan area. Marjorie was responsible for overseeing the work of five administrative assistants who supported the work of the office. This meant they would take care of such clerical matters as recordkeeping, data verification, forms processing, client scheduling, accounts payable and receiving, and the like.

Marjorie had been in this position for two years and was just now feeling comfortable with her ability to supervise others effectively. By and large, she got along well with her subordinates, and she felt that they did a reasonably good job. The only exception was Valerie Lucas. Valerie was 39 and the sole head of her household, which included two teenage children. At this point, Valerie had been with Helping Hand for almost 11 years.

In looking through her personnel file, Marjorie discovered that Valerie had never received an outstanding evaluation. At best, she received average evaluations. About six years ago, it appeared Valerie had become more of a marginal employee. She began cycling in and out of disciplinary warnings, counseling memos, and related matters. Even after all this time as an employee, Valerie had virtually no accumulated sick leave. She was often late to work by 15 minutes. She also occasionally got into shouting matches.

On this particular day, Marjorie was looking for Valerie because there had been some problems with the bus scheduling that needed to be cleared up as soon as possible. Even though it was just before lunch, there were some important deadlines and waiting riders involved. Marjorie needed Valerie's immediate help on this special task.

Marjorie saw Valerie near the filing cabinets and walked over to her, saying "Valerie, I'm glad I found you. I need you to check some of the rider schedules and bus driver alternatives on the Broadway Street bus breakdown problem. I told the clients that we would get right back to them with the solutions." She handed Valerie a form and started to walk back to her desk.

In a strong voice, Valerie said, "You're the damn supervisor, you do it." Her voice was loud enough to attract the notice of some nearby coworkers at their desks.

Marjorie was so surprised that she stopped, turned around, and responded, "What did you say?" Her voice combined disbelief and anger.
"You heard me," Valerie replied defiantly, her voice even louder. "You're the damn supervisor. You do it."

Marjorie was standing in front of Valerie. She was aware that there was now a group of employees standing nearby, staring. Valerie is staring at Marjorie. She had thrown down onto a nearby table the form Marjorie had handed her.

141

CASE QUESTION

What should Marjorie do?

The Management Training Tool Kit: 35 Exercises to Prepare Managers for the Challenges They Face Every Day, ©2012 HRD Press.
Published by AMACOM Books, American Management Association, www.amanet.org.

Case Discussion:
A "No" in the Field

Summary

Marjorie Brown supervised five administrative assistants in a transportation and housing services nonprofit organization. One of her employees was Valerie Lucas, a long-time employee with the organization. For the past few years, Valerie had been a marginal employee and often involved in various disciplinary proceedings. She would continually come to work late and argued with employees. She did an acceptable, but seldom outstanding, job.

On this day, some problems with bus scheduling required Marjorie to ask for Valerie's help. It was shortly before lunch, but there were a number of clients waiting for this problem to be resolved. Marjorie saw Valerie near the filing cabinet and directed her to help with the problem.

As Marjorie turned to leave, Valerie said in a loud voice that she would not do it. Other employees heard her and began looking to watch them. Marjorie asked for clarification. Valerie defiantly repeated what she had said. Marjorie was now face to face with Valerie, aware that a group of employees had gathered near by and were staring at them.

Answer to Case Question

What should Marjorie do?

This is a case of gross insubordination. Marjorie should remove the discussion from a public area by instructing Valerie to step into a private office. For good measure, Marjorie should ask her assistants to join them.

Marjorie should ask Valerie why she refused to do the assignment, determining whether there might be some legitimate reason for the refusal. If there is no valid reason, Marjorie should then state that unless Valerie immediately begins to work on this assignment and complete it in a timely fashion, she will be fired on the spot for gross insubordination.

If Valerie does not comply, Marjorie should then tell her that her employment is terminated and that she is to vacate the premises immediately. Marjorie and the assistant should collect her keys and any other organizational property and supervise her as she cleans out her desk. Marjorie should indicate that Valerie will hear from the Personnel office regarding future payment and related matters.

If Valerie agrees to do the assignment, Marjorie should immediately issue her a written warning notice about her behavior, with the provision that any additional insubordinate behavior will be grounds for immediate termination.

Valerie's conduct was completely inexcusable. Furthermore, because of its blatant nature, there should be no room for compromise. Not only Valerie but all the other employees must see that such behavior will not be tolerated.

Case 30 ✎

Buddy Jefferson

Background Information

Margaret Williams believed very strongly in working hard to do her best. During her four years in the Accounts Payable Department, she did just that and was rewarded with good evaluations and two promotions. Just three months ago, she had been made assistant manager of the department. This was a newly created position that involved managing the daily operations of the department's four-member staff. Margaret had immediately liked almost everything about her new job assignment, including the challenge and additional responsibility. However, she also had suspected that this promotion signaled a further deterioration of her boss's standing with the company.

When her boss, Bill Mobley, was terminated two weeks ago, she was not really surprised. The strain between Bill and the company, which had been churning beneath the surface, finally erupted, and the events that led to his release happened very quickly. As a result, Margaret was made acting manager of the department. She was told that this situation was temporary and would change when "all the dust settled." Nonetheless, she hoped and expected the promotion would be made permanent soon.

Things seemed to go well during her first week on the job. She was busy, but she liked the challenge of learning and doing new things. She thought that if the first week was any indication, managing the department would be both easy and rewarding. However, her optimistic outlook began to fade during the second week, when Buddy Jefferson entered the picture.

Just four weeks ago, Bill had hired Buddy to work on some special projects. This was two weeks before Bill was fired. At first, Margaret had limited contact with Buddy and knew very little about him or his assignments. During her second week as acting manager, though, this all changed very quickly as she started to receive complaints about Buddy from various employees in the department. She started to pay more attention to him and discovered that the complaints were well founded.

Buddy seemed to do three things that were creating problems. First, Buddy's work was often late and contained a number of errors. Even though Buddy had prior bookkeeping experience in Accounts Payable, that experience was in a different industry. Margaret knew that the systems and procedures used here were somewhat advanced and unique to this industry; anyone new to this system would have problems. On the other hand, Margaret felt he had been on the job long enough so that he should be doing better than his recent work indicated. She also knew that Bill Mobley had always done a notoriously poor job in orienting and training new employees. She gathered that Buddy was no exception and that he was most likely inadequately prepared for this job.

Buddy's second problem was, as a few of his coworkers put it, he didn't "pitch in." Rather than help answer the phones, for example, or volunteer to help someone

145

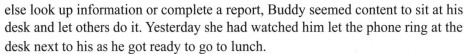

else look up information or complete a report, Buddy seemed content to sit at his desk and let others do it. Yesterday she had watched him let the phone ring at the desk next to his as he got ready to go to lunch.

Finally, Buddy did not seem to get along very well with the others in his unit and made no apparent effort to get to know them or to be friendly. Since his coworkers were busy anyway, just the slightest hint of a cold shoulder from him meant they would make no effort to meet him even halfway. Through a confrontation that Margaret had just heard about, he had even made an enemy of one of his coworkers.

Margaret knew that she needed to take some action, but was not quite sure how to proceed.

CASE QUESTIONS

1. What is (are) the problem(s)?

2. How should Margaret handle the situation?

The Management Training Tool Kit: 35 Exercises to Prepare Managers for the Challenges They Face Every Day, ©2012 HRD Press.
Published by AMACOM Books, American Management Association, www.amanet.org.

Case Discussion:
Buddy Jefferson

Summary

Margaret Williams was made acting manager of the Accounts Payable Department after her boss was terminated. In this new capacity, Margaret began to deal with a new employee, Buddy Jefferson, whom her former boss had hired just before he was let go.

Shortly after taking over, Margaret began receiving complaints from other employees about Buddy Jefferson. In looking into matters further, she found that there were three problems with Buddy:

- He submitted his work late and with a number of errors.
- He didn't seem to pitch in and help with the work in the office.
- He didn't get along well with his coworkers.

Margaret knew that her former boss had always done a poor job in orienting and training new employees. For example, Margaret knew virtually nothing about Buddy during his initial entry period.

Answers to Case Questions

1. What is (are) the problem(s)?

It would be easy to assume that Buddy is simply a poor performer and to begin the procedures to release him. However, given the circumstances of his introduction into the work group, he is showing the signs of poor orientation and integration. All of his problem behaviors can be explained as the result of not being properly managed as a new employee. Therefore, one problem is the lack of effective orientation. His performance would be considered a second problem, though, for Buddy is not performing at an acceptable level.

The real problem for Margaret is to decide whether it would be better to try to manage his orientation more effectively or to start over. This decision rests on the comparison of the relative costs of her managing him better as opposed to the costs of releasing him, hiring a replacement, and then training that replacement. In this context, the preferred course would be to try to train him better initially. If that does not work out, she still has the opportunity to pursue the second option.

2. How should Margaret handle the situation?

Assuming the solution to try at this point is to manage Buddy's orientation and training more effectively, the following steps are indicated:

1. Margaret should meet with Buddy to restart the working relationship. This would include discussing the following:

   - What the previous boss told Buddy about the job
   - Problems and difficulties Buddy is having now
   - Problems that Margaret is noticing
   - How to restart the working relationship

147

- Margaret's expected standards of performance
- An orientation and training plan

2. Margaret should initiate a more effective orientation to the job. She may need to facilitate a meeting between Buddy and his coworkers to repair any ill will. Beyond that, though, Margaret should make sure Buddy is receiving a good introduction to the firm and to its work. Buddy should be given more opportunity to interact and get to know the others in the unit, and Margaret should look for ways to include him in department activities. Assigning him to another employee who will serve as his orientation guide would be an appropriate action.

3. Finally, Margaret needs to make sure Buddy is receiving adequate training on his tasks. She should also supervise fairly closely to see if he is responding to the training and the encouragement he is receiving. If his performance does not improve, Margaret will probably need to initiate termination proceedings.

Case 31 ✍

A Wet Pain in the Neck

Background Information

About a week before Christmas, Tom Brown and his family made their annual trip to stay with his parents for the holidays. The weeks prior to the trip had been very busy for Tom and, despite his wife's good-natured scolding, he had not been able to find the time to get his hair cut. When they arrived at his parents' house, it was clear he needed a haircut. Tom's sister recommended a hair-cutting salon in a nearby shopping plaza.

Tom walked into Hair Locks about 10:00 a.m. on the day before Christmas. Much to his relief, it was not crowded. One of the two haircutters who were working on customers near the front of the salon looked at Tom and asked in a straightforward manner what he needed.

Tom snipped at the back of his head with his fingers and said, "Just a haircut." She motioned toward the rear of the shop and told him to go on back for a wash. About that time, a person who apparently was the receptionist came walking up and suggested that Tom hang his coat on the coat rack near the entrance. Tom did so, then walked to the back, not quite sure exactly where he should go, whom he should see, or what was going to happen once he got there. A diagram of the floor plan is shown below.

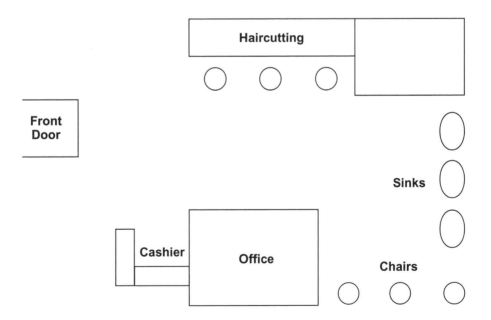

This work area included a haircutting section with a few chairs and a hair washing section with a row of sinks and chairs along the back wall. A few people were milling about. A young woman was sitting in one of the haircutting chairs, reading a magazine.

The Management Training Tool Kit: 35 Exercises to Prepare Managers for the Challenges They Face Every Day, ©2012 HRD Press.
Published by AMACOM Books, American Management Association, www.amanet.org.

No one looked at Tom when he arrived, so he just stood there, waiting, trying unsuccessfully to catch someone's eye. He leaned against a partition. After a few minutes, he started to get irritated.

Finally, the haircutter who had first spoken to Tom earlier noticed that he was waiting and signaled to the young woman reading the magazine that she should wash his hair. She casually put down the magazine, got out of her chair, and in a low-key, impersonal manner told Tom to sit in one of the hair washing chairs. She did not make any eye contact with him nor act in a friendly manner. She was rather blunt and abrupt in her actions.

After Tom sat down, the young woman wrapped an apron around his neck and placed his head back against the sink. She began washing his hair without comment. After a few moments, Tom asked her how much the haircut would cost. She flatly replied: "Fourteen dollars." Tom was used to paying nine dollars for a haircut at his hometown barbershop. While washing his hair, she lifted Tom's head, carelessly exposing his neck. A fairly large spray of water ran down his neck, soaking his shirt collar.

The young woman finished, escorted Tom to an empty chair in the haircutting section, and walked away without comment or explanation. Tom was seated next to another man whose hair was being cut. Again, Tom waited for about five minutes, not knowing what would happen next. There was nothing to read or look at.

Finally, the man next to Tom was done and went to the front desk, accompanied by the woman who had cut his hair. She went behind the receptionist's desk, seated herself in front of a personal computer, entered some information, and took his payment. He left.

She then walked toward Tom and finally spoke to him, saying she would be back in just a minute. She disappeared around the corner in back. Tom waited. After a couple of minutes, the woman returned and without introducing herself, asked Tom to move into the chair where she had been working on the previous customer.

After Tom was seated, she began straightening his apron, then realized that it was on backwards. She took it off, reversed it, and put it back on him. There was little conversation during this time. Tom's irritation with the service he was receiving had grown into outright anger.

As she picked up some scissors, she began to talk about the weather, but Tom cut her off. In an abrasive tone, Tom told her, "Wait a minute. You need to know what I want." The woman paused, somewhat taken aback. He proceeded to tell her what kind of haircut he wanted. She listened but made no effort to inquire how he had been treated so far.

She then began cutting his hair, and was very proficient in that regard. While it was not a superior cut, Tom was still pleased with the results. She dusted off Tom's head, then began applying a jelly-like substance to his hair. This last step was new to Tom, and he was not only perplexed by it, but pretty sure that he did not want it. He asked her what the substance was. She said it was a styling gel.

When the woman finished, she took off Tom's apron. They walked to the receptionist's desk, and she again seated herself at the computer. She asked Tom's name and entered the information into the computer. The system worked slowly, as she explained in a friendly tone.

150

"That will be fourteen dollars," she said. Tom was surprised. He assumed that the young woman who had washed his hair was incompetent and uninformed, and he was expecting a different price.

Tom gave her a two dollar tip. She thanked Tom for coming in and wished him a good holiday. She did not ask about the service he had received.

Tom rendezvoused with his sister and wife at the car. His sister asked how the salon was. Tom didn't hesitate to speak.

"It was very lousy service," he said. "Don't ever recommend that place to anyone again."

CASE QUESTIONS

1. Describe the various points of contact (or "moments of truth") that Tom had at Hair Locks. Evaluate the adequacy of each moment of truth. Define the standards of service that should have existed at each point.

2. How should this service cycle be managed to ensure that these standards are consistently maintained?

The Management Training Tool Kit: 35 Exercises to Prepare Managers for the Challenges They Face Every Day, ©2012 HRD Press.
Published by AMACOM Books, American Management Association, www.amanet.org.

Case Discussion:
A Wet Pain in the Neck

Summary

Tom Brown arrived in his parents' hometown shortly before Christmas. He needed a haircut and, on his sister's recommendation, went to Hair Locks, a haircutting salon in a nearby shopping plaza. It was the day before Christmas, in the morning, and there were no waiting lines. A haircutter who was working on a customer asked what he wanted. When he said he needed a haircut, she motioned him toward the rear of the salon. After hanging up his coat, he followed her instructions, unsure of what was supposed to happen next.

The salon's interior was divided into two work areas: a haircutting section and a hair washing section. A few people were milling about, and a young woman was sitting in a chair, reading a magazine. No one acknowledged his presence, so Tom leaned against a wall, feeling irritated. Finally, the haircutter who had spoken to him earlier instructed the young woman to wash his hair. She reacted indifferently to him, even coldly, and made no eye contact with him. As she washed his hair, she carelessly exposed his neck, soaking his shirt collar. Afterward, she escorted him without comment to the haircutting section, where he took a seat. Next to him, the haircutter was still working on her customer. Tom did not know what to expect.

At last, the haircutter finished with her customer and went to the front desk to take his payment. She then passed through the section, telling Tom that she would be back in a few minutes. Tom waited, growing even more irritated. She returned and asked him to move into her previous customer's chair, making no effort to introduce herself. By now, Tom was extremely angry. When she started cutting his hair, he interrupted her and bluntly told her what kind of haircut he wanted. She did an adequate job of cutting his hair, but later applied a styling gel to it without explaining what she was doing. She did not ask for his reactions then, nor when he paid her at the front desk.

When Tom met his wife and sister afterward, he told them that he had received lousy service and that his sister should never recommend that place again.

Answers to Case Questions

1. **Describe the various points of contact (or "moments of truth") that Tom had at Hair Locks. Evaluate the adequacy of each moment of truth. Define the standards of service that should have existed at each point.**

   Jan Carlson, who became president of Scandinavian Airlines System (SAS) in 1981, introduced the concept of "moments of truth" (in a book by the same name) to describe each point of contact the customer has with the business. Carlson calculated that each year, 10 million SAS customers had contact with an average of five SAS employees, for an equivalent of 50 million times that the quality of SAS would be made—or broken—in the minds of these customers. These points of contact are moments of truth because they reveal how committed the business is to providing excellent service. It is possible to use this core idea to analyze the operations of a business.

   In that framework, there were four main points of contact that Tom had with Hair Locks. (If he had called on the phone for information, that would have been a fifth moment of truth.)

The analysis of Tom's experience is listed below:

1. Entrance and welcome

   Standard: Welcome customer in a friendly manner, put the customer at ease, ask what the customer wants, move the customer to the next step as quickly as possible.

   Performance: Generally, the business performed acceptably. The welcome could have been better, though.

2. Hair washing

   Standard: Treat customer in a friendly manner, respond rapidly to customer's needs, ask for any customer requests, explain procedure, provide professional treatment without negative side effects.

   Performance: The business was a complete failure on all accounts.

3. Haircutting

   Standard: Respond rapidly to customer's needs, treat customer in a friendly manner, explain procedure, ask what the customer specifically wants, provide professional treatment.

   Performance: At best, this was a mediocre experience. The only part of the experience that would be considered positive was the actual haircut itself; all other aspects of the experience were below standard.

4. Completion of the service

   Standard: Perform competent completion of billing and collection, express thanks, ask about quality of service received, give proper response to any expression of dissatisfaction.

   Performance: Mixed. There was no inquiry about the degree of satisfaction with the service received.

2. How should this service cycle be managed to ensure that these standards are consistently maintained?

First, the manager/owner should think in terms of this four-phase service cycle and communicate standards of performance for each stage. Where necessary, employees should be trained in how to meet those standards.

Second, the manager/owner should actively watch how the service is being delivered.

Third, the manager/owner should make a much better effort to assess customer satisfaction. This should at least include inquiries at the point of payment. For example, the customer can be asked seriously and systematically about how satisfactory the service was or could be given a satisfaction card that could be left at the time of payment. It is also possible to give the customer a mail-back satisfaction card or to make follow-up calls to customers. For example, the name of the customer is obtainable from a check or credit card, and a phone number could then be tracked down. Or, if the business keeps a customer file, that information would be available through that database.

Case 32 ✍

"Well, Excuuuse Me!"

Background Information

Samson and Son Plumbing recently received a copy of the letter below from Alan Johnson. The contents of the enclosure mentioned in the letter are presented on the following pages.

Alan Johnson
123 Oak Street
Arlington, ST 55546[AQ1]

February 10, 1994

Owner or President
Samson and Son Plumbing
6680 Dobbin Road
Arlington, ST 55546

Dear Owner:

   My wife and I recently used your business services. It was a very unsatisfactory experience, and I want you to know why we will never use S & S Plumbing again. Furthermore, we will also go out of our way to counsel friends and acquaintances to avoid using your services.

   I prepared the enclosed summary of what happened during that service visit so that I would have a record of my experience. I offer it to you for your information. No reply is, of course, necessary and would be in character with the quality of service received to date.

A very unhappy customer,

Alan Johnson

Enclosure

Enclosure Summary

After recently having our main bathroom finished and a new toilet installed, we found three remaining problems: the new toilet wobbled, the shower cut-off knob dripped, and a water stain appeared on the basement ceiling tiles underneath the bathroom.

155

Because we had a coupon ad from your business, I called your office around 9:00 a.m. The woman with whom I talked was very nice, and I was pleased to learn that a plumber could come that afternoon. She called me back later that afternoon to confirm that the plumbers would arrive sometime soon.

Within half an hour or so, the doorbell rang. I opened the door to find two men waiting. I said hello and invited them into the house. The taller, younger of the two said, "S & S Plumbing." The second, older man followed him in, but made no eye contact or any other acknowledgment. Both men stood in the foyer, waiting impatiently, communicating an attitude of "Don't mess with me. Just hurry up and move it." They did not introduce themselves further or make any conversation. After no more than 30 seconds of being exposed to them, I was uneasy.

I asked, "Did they tell you what we need?"

The younger man grunted some sort of noncommittal response. There was still no comment or acknowledgment from the other man.

I continued: "Well, let me show you the projects we have in mind." I led them into the bathroom around the corner. As I started to explain what we wanted, the older, silent man walked over to the box containing the shower fixture replacement kit we had purchased. Without any comment, he opened the box and began taking it apart. He had still not looked at or said anything to me.

I was becoming more and more irked.

Without saying a word, the younger partner walked out of the bathroom and began to search for the access box to the shower pipes. He looked in the closet, which was loaded with coats. He started walking back toward the bathroom.

When he finally did speak to me, his voice was just barely audible, and at first I thought he was talking to his associate. His tone was domineering and abrasive. Because at first I didn't know he was talking to me, I didn't hear exactly what he was saying, but it was something to the effect that I had to move those coats. It came across as an insulting command.

I wheeled around and said pointedly, "Are you talking to me?" By now, I was mad and was deciding whether to throw these bozos out of the house. We all froze.

I think that the younger man may have realized that a problem was developing, and his demeanor softened slightly. I waited, then decided to go ahead. I led the younger man downstairs to see the water damage on the ceiling tiles and told him I would be removing the ceiling tiles and replacing them while he and his partner worked upstairs.

They removed their tools and supplies from their truck, then began working. During the next half-hour or so, I could hear them talking to—or rather arguing with—each other. The younger man seemed to be making argumentative, belittling remarks to the other man, who seemed to be doing his work. The quarrel seemed to revolve around how to remove the plaster standing around the pipes—whether they should just go ahead and "knock the crap" out of the plaster, ignoring any other consequences, or should take a more gentle approach. It occurred to me that the reason they may have been so rude was because they simply didn't like each other. Whatever the reason, it was extremely unpleasant to have to listen to them work together.

The Management Training Tool Kit: 35 Exercises to Prepare Managers for the Challenges They Face Every Day, ©2012 HRD Press.
Published by AMACOM Books, American Management Association, www.amanet.org.

After about 20 or 30 minutes, the older man came downstairs and, for the first time, talked to me. He said there was a problem. I followed him upstairs and found the younger man sitting cross-legged in front of the access box, gently chiseling away the plaster caked around the pipes. The older man explained that they had to remove the plaster in order to install the new fixture. However, there was a "50/50 chance" that the tiles in the shower stall might be knocked loose in the process. He wanted to know whether I would authorize them to proceed.

I asked them how difficult it would be to reset the loose tiles. He said it could be tough going and costly. I was not encouraged and wondered whether I wanted these guys doing this work. On the other hand, I knew the fixture had to be replaced, the plumbers were here, and the plaster was definitely caked around the pipes. So I told him to go ahead with the work.

The older man started to walk away. I asked whether it would make sense to put a towel in the tub to catch any falling tile. He said that if they fell, they would probably break, but then he shrugged his shoulders and added, "Why not?" Otherwise, he was completely indifferent to the tile problem. It was as if he were saying to me, "Tile is someone else's problem, like yours. It's not mine. If we break 'em, we break 'em."

After putting a towel in the tub, I left the bathroom, expecting them to break three or four tiles and leave me with holes in the shower. I returned to my work downstairs, dejected and angry. They continued working together and arguing. I concluded that the fate of the bathroom tiles was in the hands of men who could care less. They were more interested in doing the job fast than in protecting my property. I thought of what it would be like to be in the hands of a doctor who was more concerned about making a 3:00 p.m. tee-off time at the golf course than about attending fully to my needs.

During this time, I would occasionally go upstairs to see how things were going. On one visit, I found, to my surprise and relief, that there were no missing tiles in the tub. It would be nice if the plumbers had let me know.

I returned to my work downstairs. The two men upstairs seemed to be working together more smoothly, and I began to sense that they were finishing up. At one point, the older man came down to look at the ceiling/bathroom drainage problem, but did not look at it again.

Finally, the younger man called to me from upstairs. He had a dust pan in hand. The closet had been returned to a normal state, the tools and equipment were gone, and the older man was in the truck. The younger man, much more personable now, indicated they were finished. He seemed like he was ready to go, so I asked him whether I should pay him or send a check to S & S. He replied that the other guy was in the truck, writing up the bill. I followed him outside, thanking him for the work and apologizing for our old and difficult plumbing. He laughed it off, saying that it was not my fault.

I went back inside and looked in the bathroom. There was still a lot of crumbled plaster lying in the tub. The nozzle flange around the showerhead was hanging loose, and I could see small cracks in two pieces of tile near the handles. The towel I had placed in the tub was still sitting there, soggy and dirty. I waited in the kitchen.

The Management Training Tool Kit: 35 Exercises to Prepare Managers for the Challenges They Face Every Day, ©2012 HRD Press.
Published by AMACOM Books, American Management Association, www.amanet.org.

The older man returned with the bill. He led me to the bathroom and explained that they had reseated the toilet in order to stop the leak into the basement. He told me to caulk around the base of the toilet as a way to anchor it to the floor. He also told me to caulk around each of the collars around the faucet, handles, and showerhead. He also suggested using caulk on the cracks in the tile.

I pointed out to him the loose collar around the showerhead. He jiggled the head, showing me for the first time that the head itself was still somewhat loose. He advised filling the hole with caulk and then trying to sit the collar to the wall.

We chatted while I wrote the check. He handed me a copy of the invoice, and after a few more pleasantries, he left.

After my wife returned, we noticed that the pipes throughout the house sounded funny. (Obviously, during the course of the installation, it was necessary for them to cut off the main water supply.) We think—and hope—that this problem is just a temporary one due to air in the pipes. However, the plumbers left without either advising us about this or, even worse, making sure there was no problem.

Here's the outcome. The new shower fixture was installed, but at the cost of two new small cracks in shower tiles. This scenario was explained to me in advance. However, to complete the installation, it is now my job to buy caulk and put some around the collars and the toilet. The collar around the showerhead hung loose, and the showerhead itself was loose. The tub was left dirty, although the closet was cleaned. The toilet now has a new seal, but it is not clear whether that will fix the leak onto the basement ceiling. I had a very unpleasant and stressful time working with these two guys.

CASE QUESTIONS

1. What should the owner of the company do upon receiving this letter?

2. Prepare a service quality training plan for plumbers.

3. What kind of management practices should be instituted to create and maintain service quality?

The Management Training Tool Kit: 35 Exercises to Prepare Managers for the Challenges They Face Every Day, ©2012 HRD Press.
Published by AMACOM Books, American Management Association, www.amanet.org.

Case Discussion:
"Well, Excuuuse Me!"

Summary

The owner of the Samson and Son Plumbing Company received a letter from a very unhappy customer, Alan Johnson. Included with the letter was a summary of his experience with the plumbing service he had received at his house. The customer promised never to use their services again and that he would advise others to do the same.

As Alan explained it, he had several problems that needed a plumber's attention after he and his wife remodeled their bathroom. When he called Samson and Son, Alan was pleased to learn that the company could send a plumber to his house that afternoon.

When Alan answered the front door, there were two plumbers there. They were less than polite as they entered the house and were unresponsive and rude to Alan as he showed them the bathroom projects. After a very short time, Alan was just about ready to tell them to leave because of their attitudes and behavior. The younger man, who was doing all the talking, was abrasive and dictatorial. The older man made no contact with Alan at all.

Alan finished showing the tasks to be done, then went downstairs to do some work on his own. He heard the men working together, apparently in an abusive and argumentative fashion. Alan began to think that they did not like each other.

At one point, the older man told Alan that there could be a problem on one project: some tiles might be knocked loose, and they wanted his approval to proceed. Alan, feeling little choice in this bad situation, said to go ahead with the work. He expected disaster.

Finally, after about an hour and a half, the plumbers finished. They were more cordial now. However, Alan noticed that parts of the job were still left undone and that they had only partially cleaned up after their work. The older man, presenting the bill to Alan, indicated what Alan could do to fix the problems. The plumbers then left.

Answers to Case Questions

1. **What should the owner of the company do upon receiving this letter?**

   First he should call Alan Johnson and apologize. He should also offer to send over his best plumber at a time of the customer's choosing to examine the unfinished work and complete it at no charge.

   Some service specialists recommend stronger actions, like a partial or full refund or a voucher good for an equal amount of service at a future date. The owner should follow this communication with a letter of apology.

   Second he should ask the two plumbers to describe what happened during the visit before showing them the letter. When he has heard their explanations, he should let them read the letter and ask for their reactions.

   Barring a convincing rebuttal from them, the owner should clearly communicate that their behavior was inappropriate and unsatisfactory. Suitable disciplinary action may be indicated, which might include a personal letter of apology from each plumber to Alan Johnson.

Third the owner should review his company's customer service training programs. These employees should be required to attend the training. The owner should make sure the training is being conducted effectively for all applicable employees.

2. **Prepare a service quality training plan for plumbers.**

The training plan should be designed around the "moments of truth" or points of contact that the service personnel have with the customer. This begins with the phone call requesting service and extends through the post-service call assessment.

The training should establish a procedure for

- greeting the customer (on the phone or in person);
- listening to customer service requests;
- clarifying what the service will involve (including time involved, materials needed, and costs, potential hazards, and so forth);
- cleaning up after the job is finished; and
- checking up on the level of customer satisfaction after the service is completed.

The training should also include instruction in how to maintain a pleasant working climate (including how to handle disputes if there are two or more plumbers present) and how to resolve difficult customer situations. The training should combine standards of performance with practice exercises for each of these skills.

3. **What kind of management practices should be instituted to create and maintain service quality?**

There are several steps that the owner should take:

1. The selection practices used to hire plumbers should be evaluated to make sure that there is adequate attention to customer service skills (either in terms of hiring criteria or of expected job performance if hired).

2. The owner should make sure all customer contact and service personnel receive adequate training.

3. A process of regular customer satisfaction assessment should be instituted after a service call. This could take the form of a leave-behind customer satisfaction mailer or a call from the office the next day. This information should be reviewed promptly by a senior official.

4. There should be some process in place for a supervisor to make spot inspections/visits to work sites to see how the plumbers are performing.

Beyond these immediate management actions, the management of the business needs to send clear signals to all employees that quality customer service is essential and a top priority. Senior management can do this in little ways—through the actions noted above and through such things as employee recognition and reward programs that reinforce service excellence, regular training, management involvement in customer satisfaction reports, and the like. One very important way that management can signal the importance of quality service is through how it pays people. Incentive compensation programs that reward quality service are a powerful way for a company to put money where its mouth is.

Case 33 ✍

The "B" Is Back

Background Information

About 25 years ago, Bill Johnson began Johnson Properties when he bought a 20-unit apartment complex. With hard work and shrewd investments, the business grew into a multimillion-dollar company, managing over 2,000 units at 33 sites across a large regional area. To handle this volume, Bill relies on five different property managers. Each manager is responsible for the renting, maintenance, and rental collections of about six different sites. Three of the managers work out of an office at Johnson Properties headquarters, which is situated near the center of the metropolitan area in which most of the properties are located.

Now, nearing retirement, Bill Johnson has reduced his workload and responsibilities, relying on the five property managers to keep things running smoothly. With a basically hands-off approach, his normal workday is now from 9:00 a.m. to 3:00 p.m., with an hour off for lunch. Fortunately, each manager is experienced and does his or her job well.

In addition to the three property managers at the headquarters office, there is a small staff of secretaries and an accounting group. The secretaries provide the administrative support for the property managers. The accounting group is headed by Wayne Black, and includes four accounting clerks. This group maintains the accounting records for the business, taking care of accounts payable, payroll, and the like.

Molly Kurstenburg, 55, has been a permanent fixture at Johnson Properties, logging in 21 years of service. She has served as a secretary throughout that time. Two years ago, Molly was made the secretarial support for two of the property managers in the headquarters building.

During this long period of service, Molly gained a reputation among her coworkers for being a "bitch." In large part, this reputation came from her tendency to act as if she was the boss of the entire operation. An incident that occurred between Molly and her previous boss, Wendy Samikura, illustrates this problem. Before Molly moved into her current assignment, she and Wendy had ongoing problems and confrontations. One day, Molly ordered Wendy to finish up some authorization forms in 20 minutes, or else.

Wendy, busy with some other paperwork, replied without looking up: "I'll finish them when I get some time."

Molly turned and walked back to Wendy's desk. "I said for you to do them now!" she commanded.

Wendy put down her pen, stood up, and leaned across the desk. "Who do you think you're talking to? I'll do them when I'm *@%! ready." Wendy's blood went into an instant boil.

Molly leaned forward and replied: "Don't curse at me!"

At that point, both Molly and Wendy started shouting at each other. As luck

161

might have it, Bill Johnson just happened to be walking by Wendy's office, and he came in to separate them. He transferred Molly to her current job shortly thereafter. Wendy did not talk to her after that.

Over the years, it seemed that Molly had some kind of confrontation like that with everyone. She was universally disliked by her coworkers and distrusted by the property managers. In fact, the only person she seemed to get along with was Bill Johnson. She was always nice to him, getting him coffee in the morning, attending to his requests, and performing similar acts of kindness. This "Dr. Jekyll-and-Mr. Hyde" behavior produced speculation about whether there might have been some kind of affair between the two in the distant past, although there is no evidence of that now. Whether it was a love affair long ago, a current sense of loyalty to a long-time employee, or some other reason why she was nice to him, Bill Johnson offered Molly Kurstenburg some job protection.

Beth Williams, 20, joined Johnson Properties about one year ago as an accounting clerk. This is her first full-time job after graduating from high school. She is technically good at what she does, although in temperament she is very formal, aloof, and even rigid—a set of traits that contrasts with the informal atmosphere of the Johnson Properties office.

One day, Beth discovered that she needed some divider tabs for a new manual she was preparing. Not finding any in her work area, she dutifully looked around the corner of an office partition, and seeing Molly, asked her if she had any tabs. Beth had had little prior contact with Molly, although she was aware of Molly's reputation.

Molly looked up slowly from her computer, staring at Beth over the top of her wire-rimmed eyeglasses. "What do you need those tabs for?" she shot back at Beth.

Beth was not sure what to say, "Well, I, I need them for a manual I'm…"

Molly cut in, "You know those things are expensive, don't you?"

Beth stammered, "Well, I, I…"

Molly interrupted again. "They're in there," she said, pointing to a nearby cabinet.

Beth walked to the cabinet and started to open the drawer.

"Don't you dare touch that!" Molly roared at Beth. Beth froze. Molly pushed back her chair and walked over to the cabinet, stepping in front of Beth as Beth backed away. She searched through the drawer, finding a set of tabs.

"There, take these." She tossed the packet at Beth, hitting her in the face with the tabs. Beth was so angry that she started to cry. Beth then began screaming at Molly and a royal shouting match erupted that was heard throughout the office.

Wayne Black, Beth's manager, came quickly. After sizing up the situation, he sent Beth back to her desk, where she continued crying. Wayne and Molly started talking, and again a shouting match erupted—this time between Molly and Wayne.

Wayne walked back to his desk, passing Beth's desk without making a comment. Beth expected some kind of comment and could not believe Wayne did not at least ask how she was doing.

Beth followed Wayne into his office. "Well, what happened?" she asked.

Wayne barely looked up from his desk. "I took care of it," he said. "Now, get back to work."

162

"But I want to hear what happened," Beth insisted.

Wayne replied, with tension to his voice, "I told you I took care of it. Now get back to work."

Beth stood there. Her anger was now overriding the tears in her voice, "Tell me what happened or I'll leave."

Wayne stared at her, "You leave and you're fired."

Beth paused for a moment, thinking. She stared at Wayne as she replied: "I quit."

She went to her desk, got her purse, and stalked out of the office indignantly.

CASE QUESTIONS

1. Assume you are a property manager in the headquarters office. How should you respond to this situation? What can you do to correct this situation?

2. How should Wayne Black have responded to Beth?

The Management Training Tool Kit: 35 Exercises to Prepare Managers for the Challenges They Face Every Day, ©2012 HRD Press.
Published by AMACOM Books, American Management Association, www.amanet.org.

Case Discussion:
The "B" Is Back

Summary

Johnson Properties, founded by Bill Johnson 25 years ago, was a property management company that oversaw over 2,000 apartment units at more than 33 sites in a large metropolitan region. Bill was nearing retirement and relied on his property managers to run the business. Three of the property managers worked out of the same central headquarters office. The headquarters also housed a secretarial support group and an accounting function of four clerks, headed by Wayne Black.

Molly Kurstenburg, 55, was a long-term employee of Johnson Properties, having served there as a secretary for 21 years. During that time, Molly earned a reputation as a "bitch" because of her arrogant, confrontational manner with everyone.

Molly also acted as if she was in charge of everything. An incident between her and her previous boss, Wendy Samikura, illustrated the problem. One day, Molly ordered her to finish up some authorizations. Wendy indicated she would when she had some time. Molly told Wendy to do it immediately, and a shouting match ensued between the two of them. Bill Johnson happened to walk by at the time and separated them. He transferred Molly shortly thereafter. Some people in the office speculated because of Bill's tolerance of Molly's unacceptable behavior that they were lovers at one time.

One day an accounting clerk, Beth Williams, 20, asked Molly for notebook dividers. After grilling Beth about why she needed them and scaring her when she looked into the supply cabinet, Molly finally retrieved a set of dividers and threw them at Beth, hitting her in the face. Beth began to cry. Then she and Molly got into a shouting match, which was heard throughout the office.

Beth's manager, Wayne Black, came running and sent Beth back to her desk. Soon, everyone could hear him in a shouting match with Molly. Finally, Wayne returned to his office, walking past Beth without any comment. Beth, wanting some support and feedback, asked him what happened. Wayne, acting noncommittal, simply said he took care of things and that Beth should get back to work. Beth refused to leave until Bill told her what happened. A brief standoff occurred, culminating in Beth's on-the-spot resignation.

Answers to Case Questions

1. **Assume you are a property manager in the headquarters office. How should you respond to this situation? What can you do to correct this situation?**

Molly Kurstenburg appears to be a major source of friction and inefficiency in the office. Localizing and/or removing her as a source of the problem is in order.

There are several steps that could be taken in line with this goal. The most obvious step would be to have the property managers to whom she reports supervise her more carefully. They could include a disciplinary track to either promote better behavior or to remove her from the company. However, there is some good reason to assume that Bill Johnson might protect her from termination.

A second step would be to confront Bill Johnson with the problem and to ask him to manage her more carefully if he will not permit her termination. It appears that his motivation to control her is low, though, so this option may be unproductive.

The solution, then, would fall back on the actions of the managers in the group. For good or bad, some of these solutions would require an informal arrangement among the other managers in the office. They could band together to confront her with a united front whenever there are problems. They could also act to isolate her, ensuring, for example, that their employees never need to go to her for anything. They could try to reason with her to find a solution.

2. How should Wayne Black have responded to Beth?

When Wayne arrived, he should have asked Beth for an explanation of what happened. This could have been done in private, out of Molly's hearing range. He should have requested the presence of her boss to explain the situation.

When he returned to his office, he should have talked with Beth about what happened. He should have sympathized with her situation and explained what would happen next.

Case 34 ✍

Who's Telling the Truth?

Background Information

In spite of its name, the Four State Medical Supply Corporation was in fact one of the largest distributors of medical supplies and materials in the nation. Four State served hospitals and medical offices throughout the South. Joan Lloyd joined Four State as manager of the Information Systems Division not quite a year ago. Joan had been an Information Systems Department manager in a metropolitan hospital for five years prior to moving to Four State. Joan's department handled the computer information system at Four State.

The Information Systems Department was organized into three main groups: systems planning and analysis, data entry, and computer operations. All 36 people in the department shared the fourth floor of the Four State headquarters building. Even though most of the staff worked in the normal 8:00 a.m. to 4:00 p.m. shift, there was round-the-clock coverage in computer operations. The nonmanagement personnel in her department belonged to the Information Workers Union, Local 818.

During her first year on the job, Joan spent much of her time working with other managers to improve the performance of the company's information processing systems. As such, she had little daily contact with the employees in her department, although she knew them and felt that she was on generally friendly terms with each. She relied on her group supervisors to handle the ongoing supervision of employees.

One day, on her way back from a meeting, Joan ran into Brenda Upton at the elevator. Brenda worked as a data entry clerk in the Data Entry Department, which was supervised by Wilma Lane. Wilma reported directly to Joan. Brenda was also the shop steward for the unionized employees in the division, and she was known for her aggressive representation of employees in grievance matters. Brenda would advocate for an employee even when the nonunionized employees in the department had good reason to believe that the employee was wrong. This relentless pursuit to protect union members made her disliked by many in management and elsewhere.

When Joan encountered Brenda at the elevator, Brenda asked Joan if she could privately speak with her as soon as possible. Joan had some free time at the moment because of a cancelled meeting and invited Brenda into her office.

Brenda promptly took a seat in front of Joan's desk and came straight to the point: "I'm being sexually harassed by Mtombe Akilo, and I want you to make him stop. There are others who will support what I'm saying." Mtombe Akilo was a senior computer operator and supervised the midnight to 8:00 a.m. work shift.

This revelation was about the last thing Joan expected from Brenda.

"Brenda, I'm a little surprised," Joan said as she tried to recall any prior indications that there could be a problem here. "Tell me what happened."

167

Brenda looked directly at Joan as she told her: "It's happened a couple of times over the past six months or so. I'll be sitting at my terminal, doing my work, and when there's no one around, he'll rap on the glass partition, then hop on the work counter behind him. When I look up, he'll move his hips back and forth and touch himself in his crotch. It's disgusting."

Joan visualized the work area: The data entry terminals faced into the computer room, which was surrounded by a floor-to-ceiling glass wall. There was a counter just inside the wall.

Joan asked Brenda, "Well, what did you do?"

Brenda paused a moment, thinking. "The second time he did it, I walked over to the computer room and told him to stop. I was upset. But he did it a few more times. Finally, I went to his boss, Matt McWilliams, to complain."

Matt McWilliams, like Brenda's boss, Wilma Lane, was a supervisor who reported directly to Joan.

"What did Matt do?" Joan inquired.

"Oh, you know men," Brenda replied offhandedly. "He listened, then just shrugged it off. He said Mtombe was probably just kidding and that I shouldn't pay any attention to it." Brenda paused for a moment. "Mtombe did it again about two weeks ago, and that's when I decided to tell you."

After a little more conversation, Joan thanked Brenda for bringing this matter to her attention and promised to do something about it soon.

The next day, at 8:00 a.m., Joan called a meeting of Brenda, Brenda's boss, Wilma, Mtombe, and Mtombe's boss, Matt McWilliams. Joan told them that Brenda had accused Mtombe of sexual harassment and that she wanted it to stop. She pointedly asked Matt McWilliams why he had not taken any action. He mumbled something about not thinking it was a very serious problem. The meeting broke up shortly thereafter.

For the next six weeks or so, things seemed to quiet down. Joan heard nothing further and concluded that the issue had been resolved.

It was at this time, though, that Joan was invited to attend the annual meeting of the Human Resources managers, which was held to brief company managers on important policies and developments. One key issue discussed in this year's conference was sexual harassment. It was during this conference that Joan looked over the company's policy in detail. Thinking back to the incident between Brenda and Mtombe, she recognized that there were some things she had not done properly and needed to correct.

For example, under Four State policy an employee with a sexual harassment complaint should first go to his or her supervisor with the problem, unless (for obvious reasons) the employee had to go to another manager. Joan could not control or take any action on why Brenda went to Mtombe's boss instead of her own female boss. Joan could take action on another item in the policy though: the documentation of the complaint. The policy stated that all complaints of sexual harassment had to be documented within 30 days of being reported and the document then sent to Personnel.

"Better late than never," Joan thought to herself.

She dictated to her secretary an outline of what had happened and instructed the secretary to send the document to Personnel and a copy to Brenda as soon as possible.

A few days later, Personnel notified all parties—Joan, Brenda, and Mtombe—that the report had been received and would be investigated.

Brenda, clearly upset, asked to see Joan shortly after receiving the memo. Brenda's tone was belligerent and defensive: "Why did you send that report over to Personnel? I just wanted you to respond in the department."

Joan began to explain that she was required by company policy to send the report over when Brenda interrupted her: "Well if you're so concerned about policy, why didn't you send it over when you were supposed to—within 30 days? You screwed that up."

Joan was startled, but before she could respond, Brenda said sharply, "You're just trying to set me up. You and all you guys in management are just trying to get rid of me because I'm such a strong union representative. Well, it's not going to work." Brenda left Joan's office.

Before leaving work that evening, Joan sat at her desk, pondering the issue. Her thoughts turned to Mtombe Akilo. He had been with Four State for over three years, having started there shortly after immigrating to the United States from Africa. He had become a U.S. citizen two years ago. As far as Joan knew, he had consistently done a good job for the company, although his employment had not been without some stresses. For example, when he was promoted to shift supervisor, many employees in the unit complained because they did not think he was competent enough to be a supervisor; also, a little over a year ago, he found his tires slashed after a particularly troublesome disciplinary process with a few of his employees. Overall, he did not strike Joan as someone who would harass anyone, although she was aware that appearances could be very deceiving.

The next morning, Mtombe was waiting to see Joan when she arrived at her office. She invited him to take a seat. Even though Mtombe tended to be somewhat reserved, Joan could tell that he was upset. He asked Joan to remove the record of Brenda's harassment accusation from his personnel file. Joan told him that she could not do this because the matter was now in the hands of Personnel. She did offer to go with him to Personnel to discuss matters, though.

Mtombe thought for a minute, then said, "I'm really innocent. I never did what Brenda said. She's just trying to ruin me." Joan saw that Mtombe was clearly shaken by these events.

"Well, why would Brenda make up such a story?" Joan wondered aloud.

"I tell you," Mtombe answered. "It's because I wake her up."

Joan was puzzled by this, and listened as Mtombe told her his story.

Joan learned from him that Brenda's mother also worked at Four State, in the kitchen area, where the workday began at 6:00 a.m. Because Brenda and her mother lived together, they also commuted together, which meant that Brenda usually arrived at work about 5:45 in the morning. To fill the time, she would go to the dark and deserted employee lounge and sleep until 8:00 a.m., when her own workday began.

When his shift was finishing up for the night, Mtombe would sometimes stop by the lounge to get a coffee or a breakfast snack from the vending machines. On a number of occasions, he inadvertently woke Brenda up. This usually led to a bitter argument between them, and not long before Joan held the meeting on the harassment issue, Brenda

The Management Training Tool Kit: 35 Exercises to Prepare Managers for the Challenges They Face Every Day, ©2012 HRD Press.
Published by AMACOM Books, American Management Association, www.amanet.org.

told him that she was going to get even with him. Mtombe concluded by telling Joan, "Why would I mess with her? I'm afraid of her."

The next day, Joan received a letter from an attorney, indicating he was representing Brenda in this matter.

Joan stared out the window of her office. She now fully believed that Mtombe was innocent. One question after another raced through her mind: Why did Brenda wait so long to bring this to the attention of management? Why did she first go to Mtombe's boss, a male, rather than go to her boss, a woman? Why did she just want me to handle it informally in the department? Brenda obviously knows the company's policy, so why should she have been surprised when I followed it? There were just too many loose ends.

CASE QUESTIONS

1. How should Joan have handled the first report of sexual harassment from Brenda? Should she have called the meeting?
2. Given the situation as it stands, what should Joan do now?

The Management Training Tool Kit: 35 Exercises to Prepare Managers for the Challenges They Face Every Day, ©2012 HRD Press.
Published by AMACOM Books, American Management Association, www.amanet.org.

Case Discussion:
Who's Telling the Truth?

Summary

Joan Lloyd managed the Information Systems Division of the Four States Medical Supply Corporation. There were 36 people in her department, and they were organized into three groups: planning, data entry, and operations. The operations group worked round-the-clock shifts, while the typical working day for everyone else was 8:00 a.m. to 4:00 p.m. The nonmanagement personnel were members of a union, and their shop steward was Brenda Upton. Brenda aggressively represented employees before management and was disliked by many in management and elsewhere. Brenda worked in the data entry group.

One day, Brenda asked to talk with Joan privately. In the meeting, Brenda accused Mtombe Akilo of sexually harassing her. Mtombe, a recent immigrant from Africa and a newly naturalized U.S. citizen, supervised the midnight to 8:00 a.m. shift in the Operations group. Brenda told Joan that when he would see her at her workstation next to the Operations center, he would get her attention and make sexual gestures. Brenda indicated this began about six months ago. She initially told Mtombe to stop, then went to his supervisor to complain. Mtombe's supervisor, Matt McWilliams, dismissed her complaint. When Mtombe did it again two weeks ago, Brenda decided to tell Joan.

The next morning, Joan called a meeting with Brenda, Mtombe, and both of their supervisors. She told them that the harassment had to stop. For the next six weeks, she heard nothing further and assumed the matter was closed.

At that time, Joan attended an internal management meeting, where she learned that she had not followed company policy on dealing with harassment matters. When she returned to her office, she filed a report on what had happened and submitted it to Personnel. Shortly thereafter, Personnel notified all parties—Joan, Brenda, and Mtombe—that they would be investigating the matter.

Brenda met with Joan again, angry that Joan brought the matter to the attention of Personnel. She accused Joan of not following procedure and of trying to pressure her because of her union position. Later, Joan received a letter from a lawyer whom Brenda had hired to represent her.

The next day, Mtombe Akilo met with Joan. He was upset about the situation and asked Joan to remove the harassment accusation from his file. When Joan explained she could not do that, Mtombe claimed to be innocent and presented his version of events. According to Mtombe, Brenda came in early to work every day because she commuted with her mother, who worked in the cafeteria and began her job at 6:00 a.m. Brenda would go to the employee lounge and sleep until starting time. Near the end of his shift, Mtombe would go into the lounge and inadvertently wake her. An argument would ensue. Not long before the big meeting with Joan, Brenda threatened to get even with Mtombe.

Joan thinks back over Brenda's story and has questions about it. Why did she wait so long to say something? Why did she go to Mtombe's boss rather than to her own? Why did she want the matter kept within the Department? Joan now believes that there are too many loose ends, and that Mtombe is innocent.

Answers to Case Questions

1. How should Joan have handled the first report of sexual harassment from Brenda? Should she have called the meeting?

Joan's first obligation was to find out what kinds of internal procedures regarding sexual harassment existed within the company. She should have followed those procedures in this case.

Even without clear or specific organizational procedures, there is a standard routine for investigating sexual harassment claims that Joan could have followed in this case.

1. *Obtain a full account of what happened according to the aggrieved.*

   Joan should have made a written record of Brenda's claims, seeking specific dates and times of the alleged incidents. She should ask for names of witnesses. Mtombe's exact behaviors should be detailed, as well as how Brenda reacted.

   Joan should make it clear in this context that she will need to talk with others about this matter and that, even though she will do her best to be discreet, some aspects of this situation will likely become common knowledge in the department.

2. *Ascertain whether the behaviors were really unwelcome and offensive to the aggrieved, or just annoying and tolerable.*

   Joan should have Brenda clarify her reactions to the behaviors. Sexual conduct becomes harassment only when it is unwelcome, and Brenda's reactions are integral to determining the degree of the offense. Joan might also ask if there were any preceding discussions involving others who might have created a sexually oriented group atmosphere.

3. *Interview the alleged harasser and any witnesses.*

   Joan should give Mtombe a chance to respond to Brenda's allegations. This can be done without implication of guilt by stating:

   • The nature of the claims against him
   • That Joan is gathering facts and that no decision will be made until all parties have had a chance to present their sides of the story

   Joan should give Mtombe an opportunity to make any general reactions, then should probe about specific events. She should take careful notes of his replies.

   Joan should also talk to any witnesses. If no witnesses are named, she may want to talk with coworkers of both Mtombe and Brenda to inquire if there is any evidence that supports the accusations, including past incidents or a context that might have influenced events. For example, did Mtombe and Brenda ever date, or were they dating at the time? Was there a general climate at the workplace that encouraged the discussion of sexual matters, and what role did either Brenda or Mtombe play in the discussions? Were there any other conditions at play that might prompt one party or the other to lie? Joan could ask any other women in the area if they have ever been sexually harassed by anyone at the worksite.

   Remind all parties that the interviews are confidential and should be kept as such.

172

4. *Review the evidence.*

Does the testimony hang together? A claim of harassment will be more credible if Brenda's story is internally consistent, its specific details supported by the work scheduled in the department and the reports of others. A story loses credibility to the extent that there are loose ends, vague and contradictory details, conflicting reports, and other external facts that do not conform to the story as presented. Extenuating circumstances may also downgrade a story's credibility. Don't hesitate to interview people again to seek clarification of any anomalies in any of the reports.

5. *Make a decision based on the best available information. Match the discipline to the severity and likelihood of the offense.*

Write a memo to the harassing employee explaining the outcome of the investigation and what actions will be taken in response. Execute that discipline, which could take any of the following forms:

- Reminding the employee to avoid making suggestive comments
- Cautioning a work group to avoid a sexually explicit atmosphere
- Restoring lost benefits or wages to the employee
- Transferring the harasser
- Taking formal disciplinary action against the employee, ranging from a reprimand to full discharge

In this situation, Joan should reprimand Brenda's boss for not taking Brenda's claim seriously and acting accordingly.

Based on this general procedure, Joan was not well advised to call a meeting of all parties without a prior investigation.

2. **Given the situation as it stands, what should Joan do now?**

The wheels are now in motion, so Joan may have a difficult, if not impossible, time pulling the plug on what has happened. Hence, she should work closely with Human Resources from this point forward.

Given that Brenda is now represented by an attorney, Joan may not have any further options other than documenting what Mtombe told her and her new opinions about the matter and forwarding that document to Personnel.

Even so, Joan is left with certain questions that necessitate further statements from Brenda. Again, with the concurrence of counsel and Personnel, Joan might want to reinterview Brenda to determine how she would explain many of the anomalies in her story.

Case 35 ✍

A Leadership Challenge

Background Information

Mary Herzen could not have been happier when she was hired to supervise the Patient Services Department at Northside Hospital. At age 45, Mary had been in various patient and bookkeeping capacities for more than 15 years, and she enjoyed both the work and supervising others. This new opportunity came at a perfect time: just three months earlier, she had lost her job as part of a general reorganization at Central Hospital.

As Patient Services supervisor, Mary oversaw a department made up of a senior services representative and two service reps. It had taken five months to fill the position. The delay was caused in part by the internal job-posting process of notifying and interviewing internal applicants before advertising outside the organization.

Two Northside employees had applied. Both worked in the Patient Services Department. Juanita Ramirez, 32, had been with Northside for 10 years. She was the senior services rep, with over 8 years experience in this department. Sue Williamson, 26, had less time with Northside and, therefore, less experience in the function. Although both were interviewed for the supervisory position, neither was seen as a strong enough candidate for the promotion.

When Mary arrived for work on the first day, she met her boss, Chris Sapiro, after completing the new employee paperwork in Personnel. Chris was the one who had interviewed Mary and decided to hire her.

After going over some general guidelines and providing further details about the department and its personnel, Chris mentioned to Mary that two of her employees had applied for her job.

Chris continued, "I just mention that because there could be a possible problem with Juanita. I don't know, she might be resentful. Handle it the way you see best."

Chris then took her to the Patient Services Department, where he introduced her to the other employees and showed her the office. Mary began to settle in.

Later that afternoon, Mary set up individual meetings with each of the employees. She wanted to get to know them personally, learn what their job duties were and how they did their jobs. All the meetings went smoothly except the one with Juanita.

Mary could tell from the start that there would be difficulties. Juanita came in reluctantly, sat down, and did not look at Mary. Her crossed arms and unyielding stare at the ceiling conveyed the message: "Don't mess with me." Mary was barely able to get complete sentences from Juanita in response to her questions.

Mary tried to press Juanita on what her job duties and responsibilities were. After a few vague replies and more questions, Juanita said, "Look, I've told you what I do. It's your job to tell me what to do. I don't know beyond that."

This kind of exchange went on a little longer, until Mary finally said, "Juanita, if this is as well as we're going to communicate, we're going to have some real problems."

175

That seemed to catch Juanita's attention.

"Don't try to frighten me," Juanita replied tensely. Juanita was clearly chewing over something in her mind.

Mary paused, unsure of what to say next.

"The only reason you got this job is because you're Anglo," Juanita finally said. "I should have had that job. This hospital is afraid to promote a Chicano into management."

Juanita halted for a moment, her bottom lip starting to quiver. She began crying.

"I've been discriminated against…. You're the boss. You're the one who's supposed to know it all. I'm not going to answer any more of your dumb questions. You tell me what I'm supposed to do."

CASE QUESTIONS

1. Should Chris have informed Mary about the internal applicants before offering Mary the job?

2. Was meeting with each employee as part of Mary's orientation a good idea?

3. Evaluate the agenda Mary used. How could it be improved?

4. How should Mary respond to the issues Juanita is raising?

5. What are some general issues new managers and supervisors may face when assuming responsibility for a new job?

The Management Training Tool Kit: 35 Exercises to Prepare Managers for the Challenges They Face Every Day, ©2012 HRD Press.
Published by AMACOM Books, American Management Association, www.amanet.org.

Case Discussion:
A Leadership Challenge

Summary

Mary Herzen felt lucky to be hired for the supervisory position in the Patient Services Department at Northside Hospital. She had lost a similar job at Central Hospital three months earlier. Chris Sapiro was Mary's boss and had conducted the selection process. It took him five months to fill the position as a result of the internal job announcement and job-interviewing procedures.

Two employees in the Patient Services Department had applied for the supervisory job: Juanita Ramirez, 32, who had been in the department for eight years, and Sue Williamson, 26, who had less experience. Both were rejected because they were not seen as strong enough to be promoted.

Chris told Mary about this when he met with her on Mary's first day on the job. He suggested that Juanita might be a problem and told Mary to handle it the way she saw best. He then took her to the department, introduced her to the staff, and left her to settle in.

Later that day, Mary held meetings with each of her new employees. The meeting with Juanita turned out as predicted: she was defensive, uncommunicative, and noncommittal. For example, Mary wanted to learn what Juanita's job duties were, but could not get adequate replies. Finally, in exasperation, Juanita began arguing that it was Mary's job to tell Juanita what to do. Mary replied that they would have problems if this was as well as they were going to communicate. Juanita then told Mary that she had not been promoted because she was Hispanic, and accused the hospital of discrimination. She began to cry and said she was not going to answer any more questions.

Answers to Case Questions

1. **Should Chris have informed Mary about the internal applicants before offering Mary the job?**

    Yes. It is important to give job applicants all relevant information about the job for which they are applying. This is especially true for information that might be considered negative. The bulk of research in this area makes it clear that "realistic job previews" are very important for creating the most favorable initial job conditions.

2. **Was meeting with each employee as part of Mary's orientation a good idea?**

    Although Mary's idea was backed by good intentions, problems resulted. In general, individual and group meetings both have advantages and disadvantages, and whether one would work better than another for a new supervisor is a matter of personal judgment.

    One obvious advantage of a group meeting is that certain messages from the new supervisor can be given to everyone at the same time. Another advantage is that the presence of a group has the potential to pressure employees into opening up and sharing what is on their minds. In Mary's situation, a group meeting could have been especially helpful in this regard, creating an environment in which Juanita felt additional pressure to be more forthcoming.

    It should also be noted that a new supervisor can also follow up a group meeting with individual meetings, thus combining the two methods.

3. Evaluate the agenda Mary used. How could it be improved?

Again, the general intention was appropriate, although the execution was not as good as it could have been. The purpose of the introductory meetings is to initiate dialogue. Mary needed to share information as well as receive it.

A more suitable agenda would have Mary *share* information on such matters as her personal background and goals, her leadership style and practices, her priorities for the near term, and how she would like to work with the employees. She should *ask* each employee for information on their job duties, where they stand on projects, any particular problems they are experiencing, and anything else they can tell Mary that would help her supervise.

4. How should Mary respond to the issues Juanita is raising?

Mary cannot say whether in fact Juanita is correct or incorrect in her belief that she was a victim of discrimination. It is a discussion that Mary cannot win. Furthermore, she cannot prevent Juanita from taking action on her complaint if she wishes to do so. Mary therefore should not try to argue with Juanita. Indeed, Mary might simply say something to the effect that she cannot respond to Juanita's opinion but finds it difficult to believe that there was discrimination.

Instead, Mary does need to deal directly with Juanita's intransigence and belligerence. Mary should pause until Juanita is composed, then tackle this matter head on. She should make it clear to Juanita that although she cannot talk about the discrimination matter, she is concerned about Juanita's current behavior. She should indicate that she expects employees to be forthcoming in dealing with her, just as she wants to be open with them. That is, she should establish a standard of how she wants to be treated by her employees. She should share any other information about how she will supervise.

Mary should then indicate that while Juanita's behavior is perhaps understandable, given her beliefs, it is nonetheless unacceptable. She should indicate that there can be serious problems if Juanita decides to follow a course of action like this. She should present Juanita with a decision about how Juanita wants to proceed. She should then tell Juanita that they will meet again tomorrow, at which time Mary will expect a decision from Juanita.

5. What are some general issues new managers and supervisors might face when assuming responsibility for a new job?

There are several common issues facing people when they move into a management or supervisory job. These are issues beyond the traditional orientation concerns facing any new employee.

First, there is the issue of understanding what the structure of the unit is: Who is doing what? Second, there is a concern about evaluating both the functions of the unit and the personnel involved. Third, the new manager is interested in learning about any specific problems or opportunities needing quick response. Fourth, the new manager is concerned about how to begin influencing employees to receive results in line with his or her goals and priorities.

Appendixes

Appendix A
Managerial/Supervisory Pre-Training Planning Sheet ✍

To help you and the instructors get the most out of our forthcoming training programs, we are asking future participants and their managers to complete this planning sheet and return it. Your responses are confidential, of course, and will be pooled with other respondent replies, thus forming a database that will help us create training programs that are most responsive to your needs.

PART ONE: WHO YOU ARE (Check appropriate box and complete the statement.)

☐ I am the manager of _____ and I am evaluating his/her training needs. My name is _____ .

☐ I am evaluating my own training needs. My name is _____ and I supervise _____ people in the _____ department. My manager's name is _____ .

PART TWO: WHY WE SHOULD HAVE TRAINING

Listed below are a number of reasons why organizations provide training for their managers and supervisors. Place a number in the box following each statement to indicate its importance. Use this ranking system:

3 = very important reason   2 = somewhat important   1 = not important

- Our managers and supervisors know the technical aspects of their jobs, but could improve a lot at the people-handling side of managing.. ☐

- We need management education in the values and philosophy of the organization, its goals and strategies, recent history, the views of our leaders .... ☐

- We are currently facing some problems that could probably be dealt with more effectively if we receive appropriate training that addresses these problems .... ☐

- A good training program can provide a forum where participants can exchange experiences, voice concerns, and develop useful contacts .... ☐

- Effective training can more than pay for itself through the improved performance of participants as they manage and supervise their people .... ☐

- Our supervisors and managers need help in the task-handling side: time management, problem solving, planning and scheduling, handling projects, etc. .... ☐

- We need to strengthen the management team, build trust and cooperation, and get everyone working together as *one* team .... ☐

- Our managers and supervisors need a solid understanding of such concepts as leadership, authority, management style, motivation, and organizational theory .... ☐

181

The Management Training Tool Kit: 35 Exercises to Prepare Managers for the Challenges They Face Every Day, ©2012 HRD Press.
Published by AMACOM Books, American Management Association, www.amanet.org.

PART THREE: WHAT IS AND ISN'T NEEDED

On this page and the next we've listed 24 skills and abilities that are relevant in different degrees to the role of being a supervisor or manager. Your job is to rank yourself or the person you're evaluating on **Relevancy** and **Proficiency** for each factor. Circle the H or M or L in each column to indicate High or Moderate or Low.

	Relevancy	Proficiency
1. Ability to set realistic goals and standards, define performance requirements, and develop plans for tracking performance	H M L	H M L
2. Skill in communicating effectively in face-to-face situations with employees, management, customers, peers, etc.	H M L	H M L
3. Ability to conduct selection interviews that get the right faces in the right places consistent with the job, our policies, and the law	H M L	H M L
4. Skill in managing daily activities so as to balance the demands of the work (production) and the employees (people)	H M L	H M L
5. Ability to provide on-the-job training and feedback so that all employees are working at full proficiency	H M L	H M L
6. Skill in building a cohesive work team whose members are committed, motivated, challenged, and highly satisfied with their work	H M L	H M L
7. Ability to coach and counsel employees with work problems, career opportunities, and personal needs	H M L	H M L
8. Skill in disciplining, when necessary, in such a way as to restore performance without making the problem worse or causing loss of face	H M L	H M L
9. Ability to listen in depth, drawing out what isn't said, summarizing, clarifying, and organizing for future recall as needed	H M L	H M L
10. Skill in giving information (reports, instructions, news) in a well-organized, to-the-point manner—factual, objective, lean	H M L	H M L
11. Ability to ask questions effectively and get information from others in a neutral manner (i.e., clean, unbiased intelligence)	H M L	H M L
12. Skill in delegating: clear assignment, selection of right person, coaching without hovering, providing resources and support	H M L	H M L
13. Ability to manage time (of self and others) by prioritizing, controlling interruptions, budgeting, exercising self-discipline	H M L	H M L
14. Skill in methods improvement, work simplification, flow charting, process analysis, and in finding ways to work smarter and better	H M L	H M L
15. Ability to hold meetings, briefings, and conferences that are well-organized, crisp, and results-oriented	H M L	H M L
16. Skill in writing letters, memos, and reports that are clear, concise, complete, and compelling (i.e., they get acted upon)	H M L	H M L

The Management Training Tool Kit: 35 Exercises to Prepare Managers for the Challenges They Face Every Day, ©2012 HRD Press.
Published by AMACOM Books, American Management Association, www.amanet.org.

	Relevancy	Proficiency
17. Ability to make effective presentations and sell ideas in a persuasive, well-documented manner to management, teammates, etc.	H M L	H M L
18. Skill in negotiating to resolve or manage conflict as it arises concerning interpersonal relations and differences in priorities	H M L	H M L
19. Ability to manage by objectives at the work-group level (focusing on goals and standards, setting up controls, documenting progress)	H M L	H M L
20. Skill in planning and scheduling of projects and managing resources and outside people to produce results within time and budget constraints	H M L	H M L
21. Ability to interact with others on an adult-to-adult basis (and not parent-to-child: judgmental, critical, or over-nurturing)	H M L	H M L
22. Skill in problem solving: separating causes from symptoms, evaluating evidence, weighing alternatives, implementing solutions	H M L	H M L
23. Ability to think clearly and analytically, draw logical conclusions on valid premises, avoid false reasoning and fallacies	H M L	H M L
24. Skill in making decisions: list and weigh criteria, seek alternatives, assess risk, assign numerical values, select best option	H M L	H M L

If you can think of any other skills and abilities that are relevant and that we have not included on our list, please describe them in the space below.

From what you know of supervisory or managerial training programs that have been offered in the past (either here or elsewhere), what topics or course content do you feel have either been overemphasized or underemphasized?

• Overemphasized (too much time spent on these subjects):

• Underemphasized (not enough time spent on these subjects):

The Management Training Tool Kit: 35 Exercises to Prepare Managers for the Challenges They Face Every Day, ©2012 HRD Press.
Published by AMACOM Books, American Management Association, www.amanet.org.

PART FOUR: HOW WE'LL MEASURE SUCCESS

How do you believe supervisory and managerial training should be evaluated? There are ten methods of evaluation listed below. Your job is to rank the ten methods, from most desirable to least desirable.

First read the ten statements. Then decide which method is **most** desirable and give it a **10.** Find the **least** desirable method and give it a **1.** Then look for the next most desirable, giving it a **9,** and so on. You might want to use the space in front of each statement to jot down your tentative ratings, crossing them out as needed until you've arrived at the ten ratings that best reflect your views. Then enter your ten numbers in the boxes to the right.

The training program might be evaluated on the basis of:

- An end-of-course test of knowledge acquired during the program, administered on the last day .... □

- Improved attitude and performance, as reported by the participants and their managers on a questionnaire sent out after the course .... □

- Evaluation sheets filled out by the participants during the last fifteen minutes of the course .... □

- Measurements of each participant's on-the-job performance by the manager, against criteria that were generated by both parties during the course .... □

- Comments by top management, based on what they've heard and seen from participants and their managers .... □

- Attendance at class sessions, degree of participation, and extent to which outside assignments are carried out .... □

- Evaluation by subordinates (names withheld) against a checklist given to them 6–8 weeks after the course .... □

- Assessment exercise (simulations, case method) used before and after the course in order to measure proficiency .... □

- Improved performance of subordinates (reduced absences, lateness, waste, errors, complaints; higher productivity) .... □

- Ability to implement specific improvements in the work group, as taught in the course and measured 6–8 weeks thereafter .... □

> What final words of advice can you give to help us deliver a training program that will have the most and best impact on you and on the organization?

184

Appendix B
The Management Style Inventory ✍

This exercise is designed to give you some insights into your management style and how it affects others. There are ten sets of statements. Each set contains five statements about an important aspect of management style. Select the statement that is most representative of your own thinking, and give it a rating of 4. Then select the next most-representative statement, and give it a rating of 3. Do the same with the other three statements in the set. Here are the ratings:

4—most-representative; I agree strongly

3—next to most-representative of my thinking

2—next most-representative

1—next to least-representative

0—least-representative of my thinking

In other words, each of the five statements in each set will receive a different rating from 4 to 0. You may find it easiest to make your selections if you pick the most (4) and least (0) statements first, followed by your next to most (3) and next to least (1) statements. The remaining statement will then receive your only remaining rating (2).

Enter your ratings in the boxes that precede the statements. When you've completed the ten sets and entered your ratings on all fifty statements, turn to the Scoring Instructions and complete the scoring process. Then, when you've obtained your scores, read the pages titled "Interpreting Your Scores." This will help you to understand the effect of your management style on those whom you supervise.

1

Role Perception

A. I see my work group as a team on which I function as a member, bringing resources that members need to achieve their goals.

B. One of my priority roles as supervisor is to see that my people are happy in their work, since good morale is the key to productivity.

C. My style is to spell out the details of an assignment as clearly as possible, and then step back and let my employees do it with little or no help from me.

D. When the needs of my employees and the organization are in conflict, my role is to find a compromise solution that satisfies both sides.

E. I avoid a democratic style of supervision because it leads to poor decisions and reduced productivity from workers who lack the necessary experience and resources.

185

2

View of Authority

☐ A.	I regard authority, not compromise or consultation, as the prime tool of management and the ultimate source of a supervisor's power.
☐ B.	When I make a decision, I outline the reason behind it so that my employees will see the logic and accept it.
☐ C.	I'm pretty good at integrating our group goals and standards with the skills and abilities of my people.
☐ D.	I rely on precedent and past decisions, since these are a major source of my authority.
☐ E.	Sometimes the expectations and standards that come down from above are arbitrary or rigid, and I have to protect my workers from them.

3

Setting Goals and Standards

☐ A.	On many matters, my hands are tied and I act in accordance with our policies, procedures, and precedent.
☐ B.	I like my employees to "buy in" to the goals and activities that I set for them, and to feel that the ideas are theirs.
☐ C.	Close supervision is important in setting the pace, the standards, and the importance of the work at hand.
☐ D.	I avoid imposing my will on my employees; they work out their own goals and do their own planning.
☐ E.	The key to high productivity is to help my work team to develop a personal commitment to goals and standards that become theirs through involvement in planning.

4

View of Work and Workers

☐ A.	I sometimes have to serve as a "buffer" between the needs of my employees and the policies and procedures of the organization.
☐ B.	The work that I supervise is not inherently enjoyable or challenging, and a system of close control is necessary to keep people productive.
☐ C.	Each of my workers brings special resources and talents to the job, and I encourage them to arrange assignments so as to draw on each others' strengths.
☐ D.	Employees usually go along with the assignments I make, but this requires a flexible management style on my part.
☐ E.	In today's business climate, there is relatively little latitude for independent action; my role and my workers' roles are rather well defined.

The Management Training Tool Kit: 35 Exercises to Prepare Managers for the Challenges They Face Every Day, ©2012 HRD Press.
Published by AMACOM Books, American Management Association, www.amanet.org.

5

Planning and Scheduling Work

☐ A. It's important to me that my employees be involved in planning the work they perform.

☐ B. Many of the decisions I make are actually determined by well established policies or by the authorization of my superiors.

☐ C. While I must exercise control over situations, I try to get the opinions and inputs of my employees and utilize them when appropriate.

☐ D. Managers who involve their workers in decision making and goal setting are abdicating a major responsibility and inviting problems.

☐ E. Strong discipline and difficult goals set by upper management only serve to frustrate workers and the people who supervise them.

6

Giving Feedback

☐ A. I like to reward successes in a group setting, and to address failures in private with just the two of us.

☐ B. One of the reasons my people think of me as a friend is that I avoid correcting them or causing them discomfort.

☐ C. I avoid becoming personally involved in giving employee feedback; they don't like appraisals and neither do I.

☐ D. I like to see my workers giving feedback to one another on each other's performance.

☐ E. When I give criticism, employees often don't know how to take it. They're defensive and offer excuses.

7

Team Building

☐ A. My people expect me to make assignments, plan their work, and evaluate them. Overseeing their work is my job.

☐ B. I get my people to plan their work and their goals so as to achieve our organization's mission and our personal growth needs at the same time.

☐ C. As a supervisor, I know my people and their limitations fairly well, and can give assignments that are appropriate to their capabilities.

☐ D. I let my employees handle the work; they know where to find me when they need me.

☐ E. I prefer to take a consultative role, supplying ideas and then getting my people to "massage them" until they become their own.

The Management Training Tool Kit: 35 Exercises to Prepare Managers for the Challenges They Face Every Day, ©2012 HRD Press.
Published by AMACOM Books, American Management Association, www.amanet.org.

8

Implementation

A. I follow a policy of "management by exception," paying less attention to the normal flow of "business as usual" work.

B. I am "on call" to my people to help them put out fires when necessary, or when plans or goals need to be revised.

C. I expect strict and speedy execution from my people, who know that I run a tight ship.

D. I provide relatively little direction, preferring to function as a support person who creates a climate of high worker-satisfaction.

E. The quality of my group's output is enhanced by encouraging their increased participation in the setting of goals and the planning of implementation.

9

Evaluation

A. I tend to avoid discussing my employees' mistakes or failures with them, since people benefit more from encouragement and a pat on the back.

B. I try to avoid subjective evaluations of an employee's performance, and favor the objectivity of checklists and formal appraisal forms.

C. I view evaluations as learning experiences for supervisors and subordinates alike, and make them a part of every project we undertake.

D. In our daily interactions, I give feedback to my people frequently and informally. This is preferable to formal evaluation sessions.

E. In my opinion, most workers do not like to be evaluated.

10

Management Philosophy

A. I believe that workers who are going to be directly affected by a decision should participate in making the decision.

B. I'm convinced most workers would rather not take on more responsibility or authority. They look to management to plan, direct, and control the work.

C. It's important that my people accept and like me; supervisors who are not liked by their workers are usually less effective.

D. Although my door is always open to my people, I usually have minimum participation in their work unless a crisis comes up.

E. With people less and less interested in their work, we supervisors are hard pressed to get high productivity from our workers.

The Management Training Tool Kit: 35 Exercises to Prepare Managers for the Challenges They Face Every Day, ©2012 HRD Press.
Published by AMACOM Books, American Management Association, www.amanet.org.

MANAGEMENT STYLE INVENTORY

Instructions
for scoring:

This exercise enables you to assess the relative strength of five different styles of management as they relate to your own views of supervision. The five styles are listed below, next to the five lines where you should enter your totals. A detailed description of each style is included in the four pages called "Interpreting Your Scores" or "The Juggling Act Called Managing."

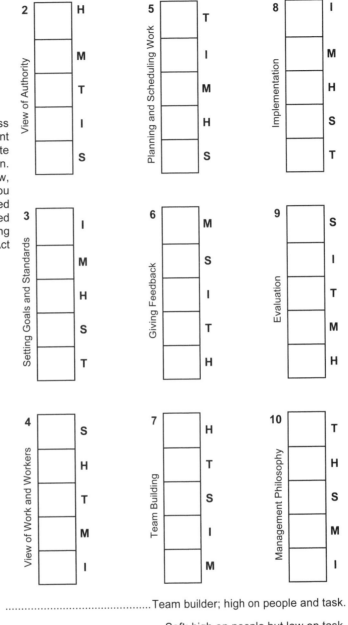

2 — View of Authority: H, M, T, I, S

5 — Planning and Scheduling Work: T, I, M, H, S

8 — Implementation: I, M, H, S, T

3 — Setting Goals and Standards: I, M, H, S, T

6 — Giving Feedback: M, S, I, T, H

9 — Evaluation: S, I, T, M, H

1 — Role Perception: T, S, I, M, H

4 — View of Work and Workers: S, H, T, M, I

7 — Team Building: H, T, S, I, M

10 — Management Philosophy: T, H, S, M, I

Sum of all ten T boxes: _____ ....Team builder; high on people and task.

Sum of all ten S boxes: _____ ....Soft; high on people but low on task.

Sum of all ten H boxes: _____ ....Hard; low on people but high on task.

Sum of all ten M boxes: _____ .... Middle of road; compromise on people and task.

Sum of all ten I boxes: _____ ....Ineffective; low on people and task.

Interpreting Your Scores

The Juggling Act Called Managing

During the first quarter of this century, the "scientific management" view of work and workers prevailed. Emphasis was placed on work measurement, production quotas, and relating wages to productivity. The second quarter of the century saw the rise of a countermovement known as the "human relations" view of work and workers. Emphasis was placed on asking workers for their opinions, getting more employee involvement in company activities, and meeting the social and psychological needs of workers, as well as their financial and physical needs.

These two schools led managers in the 1950s and 1960s to see leadership styles as an "either/or" dichotomy. A manager was either autocratic or democratic, authoritarian or participative, parent-child or adult-adult, Theory X or Theory Y. This focus on extremes led many managers to conclude that the human relations view (people-centered management) is preferable to the scientific management view (production-centered management). This preference has historically been the bias of instructors who have taught management theory (and who have rarely had to meet deadlines, payrolls, and the harsh realities of a production line). However, many other managers concluded that neither alternative was acceptable, and that a manager does not have to be "hard" or "soft" to be effective.

In the 1970s a fresh approach to management style emerged. Known as "situational leadership," it has become the prevailing view today. It began with the work of Robert Blake and Jane Mouton on the "Managerial Grid" and was picked up by Kenneth Blanchard and Paul Hersey, William Reddin, Jay Hall, and other behavioral scientists whose research and instruments have made grid theory the best known leadership concept in the literature today.

Situational leadership, simply put, is an acknowledgment of the futility of seeking a universal model to explain supervisory/managerial behavior. A manager's style is dynamic, not static. It must be responsive to a variety of situational factors (twelve of which are listed on the next page). Thus, a manager's behavior can be shown on a grid, where concern with people (relationships) and concern with tasks (production) are the two major forces working on a manager. These two should be kept in balance over the long run, although the needs of any given situation might push a manager toward the upper left or lower right corner of the grid.

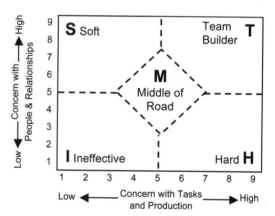

The Management Training Tool Kit: 35 Exercises to Prepare Managers for the Challenges They Face Every Day, ©2012 HRD Press.
Published by AMACOM Books, American Management Association, www.amanet.org.

FACTORS AFFECTING YOUR STYLE AS A SUPERVISOR/MANAGER

FACTOR	DESCRIPTION
Personality	Your genes and your upbringing have made it easier for you to behave in some ways than in others.
Values and Assumptions	Your values and perceptions of people and situations are the filters through which all your actions and decisions are passed.
Expectation of the Work Group	You must respond to the values and needs of your workers. Supervisors in strongly organized (union) settings display different behaviors in non-union settings.
Relationships Downward	The trust and openness of downward communications influence (and are influenced by) your leadership style.
Relationships Upward	The models and mentoring that you are or are not receiving from above will shape the way you behave in turn.
Organizational Structure	As companies become more complex and adopt a "matrix" type of structure, supervisors must learn how to negotiate, compromise, adapt, and accommodate.
Nature of the Work	Some tasks are pleasant; others less so. Some work stations and environments make supervising easy; others less so.
Culture and Climate	The philosophy of the organization, its norms and culture, its climate and tempo all affect how you supervise.
Expectations of Society	Employees must respond to the larger environment: expectations of the public, demands of consumers, the changing work ethic.
Degree of Pressure	Given time, you can invest in the coaching and development of workers. But under pressure for immediate results, you are pushed toward a "hard," or task-oriented style.
Level of Your Employees	In general, better educated and/or more experienced workers respond to a more participative style, while inexperienced and/or less educated workers need closer supervision. As your employees develop, so should your style.
Rewards and Reinforcers	All organizations have formal and informal systems for rewarding and punishing behavior—positive and negative sanctions, reinforcers, and constraints. These flow downward from superiors, sideways from peers, and upward from workers.

191

The Management Training Tool Kit: 35 Exercises to Prepare Managers for the Challenges They Face Every Day, ©2012 HRD Press.
Published by AMACOM Books, American Management Association, www.amanet.org.

H   **Hard
Style**   **Seen by others as authoritarian, autocratic, "hard" Theory X,
                                 judgmental parent-child, "taskmaster," critical.**

This manager places production before people. "Getting the work done is more important than being popular or keeping everyone happy," says the **H** supervisor. This style is appropriate in emergency situations, such as when a manager must get employees out of a burning building, when a platoon lieutenant must get his men to move across a field under fire, or when a football coach must call the plays for a team that is trailing in the last quarter with five minutes left to play.

The **H** style is likely to be found where there has been a militant union or where the work is routine and monotonous, or where workers are new, inexperienced, and less educated. It might also prevail where the workers expect it and regard it as a sign of strength (e.g., in traditionally male-dominated jobs: truck driving, construction, lumbering, oil rigging, marine-maritime, etc.).

Most managers find that the **H** style can be effective **in the short run** to manage an unusual, one-time, extraordinary effort—military combat, a four-alarm fire, a sales manager running a campaign to get lagging sales up by the end of the quarter. But if **H** is the prevalent style of a supervisor, employees will become dependent and are likely to respond to the "carrot and stick" of their boss rather than to the situation itself. And when they do become bruised or "bent out of shape," the supervisor is not likely to be very effective in restoring harmony.

S   **Soft
Style**   **Seen by others as permissive, democratic, "soft" Theory X,
                                 nurturing parent-child, "country club manager," pampering.**

This manager is permissive, placing people before production. The S supervisor believes that "Overemphasis on productivity, objectives, and standards will merely turn people off, and they won't do their best work . . . At least, it won't be as good as you'll get by taking care of your people and being popular with them." This style is appropriate in situations where creativity, individuality, and relationships are important. A dean of faculty or department chairman at the university, the head of a team of research scientists, the supervisor of volunteers in a charity or social welfare agency, or the president of a local service club (Woman's Club, Elks, etc.) are positions where a soft style might be preferable.

The **S** style is likely to be found in situations where relationships are more important than output. But the **S** style will emerge whenever the supervisor has a strong need for acceptance (need to be liked, to be popular, to "make up" for an unpopular prior action). Such supervisors tend to overlook human error: "Everybody makes mistakes. If he does it again, we'll have a talk." Unfortunately, this increases the probability of future errors, which tends to fuel the supervisor's belief that people depend on him or her to correct them and make things right.

Both the **S** and **H** managers are Theory X managers in that both expect less of subordinates than they are capable of. The Hard manager sees workers as incompetent or lazy, while the Soft manager sees workers as prone to make mistakes or as feeling "put upon" if extra demands come along. Thus, both the **H** and **S** managers end up doing much of the work themselves rather than delegating it.

M   **Middle-of-the-Road
Style**   **Seen by others as compromiser, manipulator, highly political,
                                 "good guy," juggler.**

This manager believes that it's important to push for productivity, until people begin to feel "put upon" or abused. Then the manager "makes peace" or "buys time" by paying some attention to relationships and ego needs. The high **M** believes "It's important to plant the seeds of change with employees so they'll come up with ideas and feel a degree of ownership. They want to feel in on the decisions."

This style is manipulative. The manager is see-saw, balanced on the thin edge of trying to get the job done and keeping people happy. The high **M** style is quite common and can be effective if the manager has sound judgment (better than the group's) and enough charisma and personality to get people to trust their leader. But the danger faced by high **M** supervisors is that they might be seen as insincere or manipulative. When this occurs, the supervisor's effectiveness will diminish rapidly.

The **M** supervisor believes that the needs of the organization and its employees are inherently in conflict. Thus, this supervisor becomes a compromiser, a referee, a juggler of advantages. ("I owe you one; I'll make it up to you next week.") Rather than seek the best situation from either a

The Management Training Tool Kit: 35 Exercises to Prepare Managers for the Challenges They Face Every Day, ©2012 HRD Press.
Published by AMACOM Books, American Management Association, www.amanet.org.

production or a people standpoint (since this would take its toll on the opposite dimension), the high **M** tries to find a position that is in between—something that is halfway acceptable.

The high **M** supervisor prefers one-to-one relationships with subordinates, which means that members of the work group usually do not function as a team. This supervisor often plays politics, both downward with subordinates and upward with the boss and upper management. Indeed, to the high **M,** it is more important to do what is expedient (acceptable and workable) then to do what is best for production and people.

I
Ineffective Style	**Seen by others as abdicating, impoverished, impersonal, highly bureaucratic, paper shuffler.**

This manager, like the high **M,** sees a basic incompatibility between production needs and people needs. However, rather than seeking compromise, high **I** managers tend to back off and abdicate. They are reactive rather than proactive. They respond rather than provide leadership. They keep busy writing "C.Y.A." memos and looking up policy and procedures. They maintain a low profile and believe in the value of not rocking the boat.

In some settings, the high **I** can be effective. Some departments or work units require a high attention to detail or to well established, tightly defined procedures (e.g., a quality control lab, accounting, purchasing, payroll, the military). At other times the high **I** style may emerge in response to dysfunctional organizational actions (e.g., where the supervisor is less competent than the employees who proceed on their own, or where the organization is highly bureaucratic, or where feather-bedding creates jobs and work units that have no functional utility).

The high **I** manager has a strong need for security, and avoids risk at all costs. This manager avoids giving personal opinion, citing instead the organization's policy, often by chapter and verse. This manager engages in "we-they" thinking on downward communications: "They say we have to clean up the situation by the 15th." And on upward communication, the high **I** is likely to blame the troops for any failures or shortfalls: "Well, with the kind of employees we're getting . . . ."

In the long run, no profit-oriented business can exist for long with a high **I** style. However, the individual high **I** manager has tenacity and an ability to survive, especially under a management where "no one is ever fired."

T
Team Builder	**Seen by others as participative, catalyst, coach, integrator, Theory Y, adult to adult.**

This manager shows maximum concern both for people and production, and is the most effective style one can have. There is no inherent conflict between the needs of the organization (production) and the needs of the workers (good relationships). Indeed, most people come to work expecting to be challenged.

New problems, decisions, and goals are what a job is all about. They make the work interesting and provide the flame to temper each worker's steel, the fuel for personal growth and development. As the high **T** puts it, "My aim is to create a work environment that integrates individual creativity, high productivity, and job satisfaction. By building a team, my people can learn how to play the game and win through teamwork. It's they who will take me to our organization's superbowl . . . not vice versa.

The high **T** makes frequent use of words like: joint goal-setting, accomplishment, contribution, challenge, mutual benefit, orchestrate (or integrate), tracking of progress, rewarding performance. The goal of the high **T** is to foster participation and employee involvement in the planning of work so that everyone in the work group has an opportunity to invest of themselves and find meaning, commitment, purpose, and opportunity for personal growth and development in the group's work.

To achieve this end, the high **T** manager is in the game for the long run. Sometimes short-term efficiencies or gains are sacrificed for long-term effectiveness, such as in delegating to party B a job that could be done quicker and better by self or party A. Other styles "come naturally" and are reactive; the high **T** style is proactive and must be cultivated. But over time it is the most satisfying and the most productive.

The Management Training Tool Kit: 35 Exercises to Prepare Managers for the Challenges They Face Every Day, ©2012 HRD Press.
Published by AMACOM Books, American Management Association, www.amanet.org.

Appendix C

Self-Inventory of Managerial Responsibilities ✍

Name: _____   Orgn/Dept: _____

This exercise is designed to provide information about the responsibilities of managing and supervising, and how they divide up between you and your boss. You'll fill out one copy on yourself using the next two pages of this inventory; the boss will also fill out a copy that you'll provide.

There are 40 items. Please respond to each. Some of the duties form a major part of your day. Others are performed periodically: perhaps once a week, or monthly, or quarterly. Under the "Time Spent" column, indicate the percentage of time you spend on each item on a monthly basis. If a particular item is not part of your job, indicate this by filling in a zero. Round off percentages to the nearest whole number.

Some of the responsibilities will overlap others. Therefore, you should not expect your "Time Spent" percentages to add up to 100; they will exceed it. Don't worry about this overlap, as it would be almost impossible to generate a list of mutually exclusive responsibilities. For example, item 25 probably overlaps with items 5 and 36. Rather than try and avoid the overlap, begin by acknowledging that your total will exceed 100%.

In the last three columns, indicate by percentage how each responsibility divides between you and your boss or others who share in it. For example, read item 1 ("Interview new non-exempt [non-supervisory] employees"). Let's assume that you share this with your boss. Anyone who is hired into your department must be interviewed by each of you. The percentage would thus be 50 for you ("Subordinate" column) and 50 for "Subordinate's Boss." If you had a personnel manager doing the initial screening interview before the applicant got to you and your boss, and each of you were more or less equally responsible for the final decision, then the figure would be approximately 33% in each of the three columns. Now let's change our example and assume that your boss does not interview those whom you hire, but you do, along with Personnel. The figures across the three columns in this case would read 50-0-50. (The three figures you enter for each item must total 100, unless *no one* is performing the function, in which case you must enter a zero in each column.)

On some items you may have full responsibility (100-0-0). On others, your boss may shoulder it fully (0-100-0). However, many of the items are divided between you. It's important that the two of you discuss your individual entries for each of the 40 items. While it is not necessary that the two of you agree on how your duties and responsibilities divide, it *is* essential that you understand the reasons behind your differences. That's why you should ask your boss to complete this form.

Each of you should complete the exercise independently. Then the two of you should get together and compare entries, paying particular attention to those items where you differ from your boss by, say, 20 or more percent (e.g., you said 50-50 and your boss said 75-25). Also, after you have established how things *are* divided between you, spend some time on how things *should* be. That is, should any of the percentages be changed in the light of this exercise?

Bring both copies with you to your next group meeting, where we'll discuss and analyze and compare results. (Remember to calculate the average percentages just below item 40.)

195

The Management Training Tool Kit: 35 Exercises to Prepare Managers for the Challenges They Face Every Day, ©2012 HRD Press.
Published by AMACOM Books, American Management Association, www.amanet.org.

SELF-INVENTORY OF MANAGERIAL RESPONSIBILITIES	TIME SPENT	WHO HAS THIS RESPONSIBILITY OR ACCOUNTABILITY?		
	%	% Subordinate	% Subordinate's Boss	% Other
1. Interview new non-exempt (non-supervisory) employees.				
2. Submit reports on the performance of non-exempt personnel.				
3. Contact employees who are excessively absent or tardy.				
4. Handle correspondence with those outside the company.				
5. Communicate policies, methods, and procedures to subordinates.				
6. Establish policy for my work group.				
7. Make progress reports to management (middle or top).				
8. Conduct disciplinary interviews with subordinates.				
9. Establish on-the-job training programs for my subordinates.				
10. Prepare checklists or rating sheets for use in daily supervision.				
11. Counsel employees on career and future growth potential.				
12. Conduct exit interviews with employees who leave.				
13. Maintain records on employee output and volume.				
14. Determine and control the quality of work.				
15. Decide when a new job position (employee) is needed.				
16. Deal with union representative(s).				
17. Conduct performance appraisals with non-exempt employees.				
18. Determine who will be promoted and when.				
19. Recommend and/or develop the departmental budget.				
20. Determine which employees will attend training sessions.				

The Management Training Tool Kit: 35 Exercises to Prepare Managers for the Challenges They Face Every Day, ©2012 HRD Press.
Published by AMACOM Books, American Management Association, www.amanet.org.

SELF-INVENTORY OF MANAGERIAL RESPONSIBILITIES	TIME SPENT	WHO HAS THIS RESPONSIBILITY OR ACCOUNTABILITY?		
	%	% Subordinate	% Subordinate's Boss	% Other
21. Develop job descriptions for non-supervisory personnel.				
22. Coordinate work flow between departments.				
23. Recommend salary increases for non-exempt employees.				
24. Organize and direct the work of non-supervisory personnel.				
25. Conduct group meetings with my work team.				
26. Recommend improvements in the work environment.				
27. Resolve conflicts among subordinates.				
28. Offer ideas for improvement of my department to management.				
29. Prepare memos and letters related to our department.				
30. Establish most efficient method of distributing and assigning work.				
31. Determine procedures and methods for getting the work done.				
32. Schedule vacations for non-supervisory personnel.				
33. Perform work of subordinates when quality or quantity lags.				
34. Give remedial training when work is below par.				
35. Dismiss or fire employees for poor performance.				
36. Give orientation to new employees about your department.				
37. Set up or maintain a cost-control system.				
38. Counsel employees on personal and work-related problems.				
39. Set work goals and standards for non-supervisory personnel.				
40. Give warning notifications or suspensions as needed.				
Average Percentage (total of 40 items divided by 40)				

34.3

The Management Training Tool Kit: 35 Exercises to Prepare Managers for the Challenges They Face Every Day, ©2012 HRD Press.
Published by AMACOM Books, American Management Association, www.amanet.org.

QUESTIONS

This series of questions should be completed by the subordinate *after* meeting with the boss. Of course, the answers should be based on the discussion and analysis of differences that took place when you compared the two forms.

1. What were the areas of responsibility in which you differed by 10% or more in the "Time Spent" column?

2. Why do you think there were differences between the two of you on how you allocate your time?

3. What action steps did you both agree would be required to correct these differences?

4. What were the areas of responsibility in which you differed by 20% or more in the "Who has this responsibility/accountability?" columns?

5. Why do you think there were differences about who has these responsibilities?

6. What action steps did you both agree would be required to correct these differences?

7. How would you interpret the distribution of percentages shown at the right?
   What does it imply about the subordinate? His or her boss?

% Subord.	% Boss	% Other
10	*80*	*10*

8. When you and your boss each calculated your Average Percentage, did you have about the same distribution (within 10%) for all your responsibilities taken together? Why or why not?

9. How would you interpret the distribution of percentages shown at the right?
   What does it imply about the subordinate? His or her boss?

% Subord.	% Boss	% Other
80	*10*	*10*

10. What is the main thing you learned from this exercise with regard to your supervisory role in your organization?

The Management Training Tool Kit: 35 Exercises to Prepare Managers for the Challenges They Face Every Day, ©2012 HRD Press.
Published by AMACOM Books, American Management Association, www.amanet.org.

Index